CON

Map references are denoted in the text by ❶ Central London ❷ West End
❸ Bus Map ❹ Tube Map ❺ Theatreland (p.29) ❻ Central London Overview

london places to see

London has to be the liveliest, grooviest, most enticing, most entertaining, most cosmopolitan city on Earth. 2,500 years in the making, it has everything the modern traveller could possibly want: superb architecture (St Paul's, the Gherkin), a world-class arts scene (the West End theatres, the South Bank), chic restaurants (The Ivy, the OXO Tower) and fantastic shopping (Carnaby Street, Knightsbridge). There are ground-breaking museums (British Museum, Science Museum) and beautiful parks (St James's Park, Hyde Park) – London boasts more green spaces than any other major capital. Culturally diverse, multi-racial and endlessly fascinating, London has a character and vibrancy not found anywhere else.

see it places to see

BBC Broadcasting House ② 1D

Take a tour behind the doors of Britain's first purpose-built, now renovated and modernised broadcasting centre, with its Art Deco mosaic floor and restored Radio Theatre. *Adm. Monthly tours on a Sun. Pre-booking essential. Portland Place W1A, T: 0370 901 1227, www.bbc.co.uk/tours*

British Museum ② 1G

Children and adults alike flock here to see the huge Egyptian collection of ancient mummies and the Rosetta Stone. The famous Elgin Marbles from the Parthenon in Athens also reside here among hoards of world treasures collected by explorers. One of the highlights of this vast repository has to be the stunning glass-roofed Great Court, the largest covered public square in Europe. In its centre, have a peek at the beautiful blue and gold ceiling of the huge round reading room. *Open 10am-5.30pm daily (till 8.30pm Thu & Fri, Great Court open till 11pm Thu-Sat). Great Russell Street WC1, T: 020 7323 8000, www.thebritishmuseum.org*

The Great Court in the British Museum

Buckingham Palace ② 7D

Standing imperiously at the end of The Mall, this grand 19th-century structure is the official residence of the Queen. Each summer the Palace opens its doors to the public for guided tours of its State Rooms (including the fabulous Royal Picture Gallery) and gardens. Don't miss the pageant of Englishness with the Changing of the Guard, which takes place daily in front of the palace at 11.30am May-Jul, alternate days Aug-Apr. *Adm. Open 9.45am-6pm daily Aug-Sep (last entry 3.45pm).* St James's Park SW1, T: 020 7766 730 www.royalcollection.org.uk

Chelsea FC Museum ① 6B

Football memorabilia from past sta and fans chart the highs and lows more than 100 years of Blues histo There's a trophy cabinet and fun interactive displays where you can pick your greatest XI, see the best-ever goals scored or send a video message to anywhere in the world *Adm. Open 10.30am-4.30pm daily. Stamford Bridge SW3, T: 0871 984 1305, www.chelseafc.ce*

4

Churchill Museum & Cabinet War Rooms ❷ 7F

...pened in 2005, this is the country's ...st museum dedicated to the great ...WII leader, Sir Winston Churchill. ...'s set next to the underground ...unkers that were the British ...overnment's headquarters during ...e war. The map room, phone ...om and Sir Winston's bedroom ...ve been preserved exactly as they ...ere left at the end of the conflict. ...dm. Open 9.30am-6pm daily. Clive ...eps, King Charles Street SW1, ...020 7930 6961, cwr.iwm.org.uk

...anging of the Guard at Buckingham Palace

Covent Garden ❷ 3H/❺

Once the site of a huge fruit and veg market, Covent Garden *(see p.18)* is now a lively, cosmopolitan centre of culture, creativity and cafés. Its former market buildings house an exciting mix of cool and quirky shops, restaurants, bars and museums (including the excellent London Transport Museum *(see p.8)*), while its pedestrianised spaces attract huge crowds watching exuberant jugglers, acrobats, clowns and mime artists. Weekends in Covent Garden are the busiest. *www.coventgardenlife.com*

Courtauld Gallery ❷ 4H

Home to the UK's most impressive collection of Impressionists including Monet, Manet, Renoir, Degas, Gauguin, Cézanne and Van Gogh, this intimate gallery also displays some superb works by Michelangelo, Botticelli and Rubens. Located at Somerset House *(see p.12)*. Adm. Open 10am-6pm daily. Free entry 10am-2pm Mon. Somerset House WC2, T: 020 7848 2526, www.courtauld.ac.uk/gallery

Dalí Universe ❷ 7H

Surreal bronze works by the Spanish artist, Salvador Dalí, are displayed in the County Hall Gallery. This is the largest collection of his sculptures in the world. On display are also some of his surreal hallucinatory images of melting clocks and dreamlike landscapes as well as his Mae West Lips sofa. *Adm. Open 10am-6.30pm daily. County Hall, Westminster Bridge Road SE1, T: 0870 744 7485, www.daliuniverse.com*

Greenwich ❶ (Greenwich inset)

There are few more charming places in London than Greenwich. Set on

the river, it's a district with a rich maritime history and a staggering architectural heritage. Christopher Wren, Nicholas Hawksmoor and Sir John Vanbrugh have all contributed to the Greenwich skyline, which has been designated a World Heritage Site by UNESCO. Its status as the home of time – this is the site of the Prime Meridian or the line of 0° longitude at the Old Royal Observatory – led to it being picked as the venue for the nation's

Dalí on the South Bank

millennium celebrations. At weekends, the bustling crafts or antiques markets (*see p.22*) attract visitors from all over. The former tea clipper, the *Cutty Sark*, sitting on the waterfront, was damaged by fire in 2007 – plans are in hand to restore her. *T: 020 8854 8888, www.greenwich.gov.uk*

Houses of Parliament & Big Ben ❷ 7G

Laid out around Big Ben – its much-loved and over-photographed clocktower – the neo-gothic Palace of Westminster (as it's officially known) is the great icon of British democracy. Staring benignly across the river Thames, it's been the seat of government for centuries. The exquisitely preserved 11th-century Westminster Hall is all that remains of the early building. *To watch a debate from the House of Commons Visitors' Gallery, you must queue from 2.30pm onwards Mon-Tue, from 11.30am Wed, from 10.30am Thu and from 9.30am Fri. Guided tours of the building itself can only be taken during the summer recess from Jul-Sep.*

Book in advance. Parliament Square SW1, www.parliament.uk

Hyde Park ❷ 3A-6B

Hyde Park, the city's green and pleasant heart, is London's largest open space. This grand expanse of grassy lawns, trees and flowerbeds laid out around the Serpentine – a snaking, duck-filled lake – where rowboats can be hired. The controversial Diana, Princess of Wales Memorial Fountain lies on the edge of Hyde Park next to Kensington Gardens (*see p.7*). In summer, the park comes to life with pop concerts and the BBC Proms (*see p.61*), open air swimming at the lido and guided walks. *Open 5am-12midnight daily. www.royalparks.gov.uk*

Imperial War Museum ❶ 5F

This excellent museum successfully strikes a balance between gung-ho displays of military hardware – tanks, planes and missiles – and exhibitions showing the human cost of war: check out the Trench Experience, the Blitz Experience and a new two-floor exhibition on the Holocaust. *Open 10am-6pm daily. Lambeth Road*

E1, T: 020 7416 5320,
www.iwm.org.uk

Kensington Gardens ❶ 3B-4B

This huge royal park was in fact part
of Hyde Park (see p.6) until William III
bought it in 1689 to live in and had
Kensington Palace (see below) built.
Next to the palace is a huge children's
playground dedicated to the memory
of Princess Diana, with a pirate ship
and tepees. The Albert Memorial (see
box, right) lies at the southern side of
the gardens. Open 6am-dusk daily.
www.royalparks.gov.uk

Kensington Palace ❶ 4B

The former home of the "People's
Princess", Princess Diana, as well as

Front Gates at Kensington Palace

the childhood home of Queen
Victoria, Kensington Palace houses a
permanent collection of the grand
Royal Ceremonial Dresses from
18th century to today. An exhibition
of 12 of Diana's dresses is on
display until February 2010. In the
summer, the beautiful sunken
gardens are a sight to behold. Adm.
Open 10am-6pm daily Mar-Oct,
10am-5pm daily Nov-Mar. Kensington
Gardens W8, T: 0844 482 7777,
www.hrp.org.uk

Leicester Square ❷ 4F/❺

At the heart of London's
entertainment district, Leicester
Square hosts most of the UK film
premieres in one of four cinemas. Buy
cut-price theatre tickets at the tkts
booth (see box, p.28) in the corner.
Wander a few streets into London's
Chinatown and stop off for a bite to
eat (see p.40), or check out the bars in
Soho before dancing the night away
in one of London's top nightspots
back at the up-all-night Square.

London Aquarium ❷ 7H

Huge million-gallon tanks filled with
tropical fish, seahorses and sharks

Remembering Albert

During World War II, this
grand, gaudy, gold-plated
statue of Queen Victoria's
beloved husband, Albert, was
painted black to prevent it
from being targeted by enemy
planes. Sitting on the southern
edge of Kensington Gardens,
it has been returned to its
former splendour.

now replace desks in County Hall, the former headquarters of the Greater London Council. The offices have been transformed into a state-of-the-art aquarium where a vast array of marine life now lives. The building also contains a museum dedicated to the great Spanish Surrealist, Salvador Dalí (see p.5). *Adm.* Open 10am-6pm Mon-Fri (last admission 5pm), 10am-7pm Sat-Sun. *County Hall, Westminster Bridge Road SE1, T: 020 7967 8000, www.londonaquarium.co.uk*

Powder Blue Tang at the London Aquarium

London Dungeon ❶ 4H

Gruesome dioramas and scary interactive exhibits combine in an overview of a gory historical past covering events such as the Great Plague and Jack the Ripper murders. The fairground-style attractions include the world's largest mirror maze. *Adm.* Book online for up to 50% discount. Opening times vary. *28-34 Tooley Street SE1, T: 020 7403 7221, www.thedungeons.com*

London Eye ❷ 6H

On a clear day, from the top of the London Eye, you can gaze over more than 40km (25 miles) of London's rooftops. Teetering on the south bank of the Thames by Westminster Bridge, the gently revolving spokes and 32 pod capsules make up the largest big wheel in the world. *Adm.* Buy online for 10% discount. Open 10am-9pm daily Jun-Sep, 10am-8pm daily Oct-May (ticket office opens 9.30am). *Jubilee Gardens SE1, T: 0870 500 0600, www.ba-londoneye.com*

London Transport Museum ❸ 3H

Reopened in Spring 2007 after a massive refurbishment, this lovely museum hides in the corner of Covent Garden. Charting the history of the capital's transport system with full-size old buses and tube trains, it is a must-see, even if you only buy your souvenirs from the excellent shop outside with underground station logo gifts and vintage transport posters (see p.24). Open 10am-6pm Sat-Thu, 11am-9pm Fri. *Covent Garden Piazza WC2, T: 020 7379 6344, www.ltmuseum.co.uk*

London Zoo ❶ 1D

The world's first 'scientific' zoo is home to a huge collection of animals from squirrel monkeys and wolves to elephants, giraffes, snakes butterflies and parrots. Don't miss penguin feeding time at 2pm daily.

Saatchi Gallery ❶ 5D

Charles Saatchi has moved his acclaimed gallery of unseen, new contemporary art to the Duke of York's Headquarters on King's Road in Chelsea in 2008. *T: 020 7823 2363, www.saatchi-gallery.co.uk*

ook out for the 'Web of Life' uilding, an incredible piece of rchitecture, and enjoy an up-close ew of lowland gorillas in the xciting £5.3 million Gorilla ingdom exhibit. *Adm. Open 0am-5.30pm Mar-Oct, 10am-4pm ct-Feb. Regent's Park NW1, 020 7722 3333, www.zsl.org*

Canalboat to the Zoo
A fun way to arrive at the zoo is aboard a canal barge. The London Waterbus Company organises trips from Camden Lock to Little Venice along Regent's Canal, stopping at the zoo. *Apr-Sep daily (weekends Oct-Mar), T: 020 7482 2660, www.londonwaterbus.com*

ladame Tussauds & the ondon Planetarium ● 2D
hen Madame Tussaud arrived in ngland from France in 1802 carrying ith her a small collection of wax asks modelled on the more notorious ctims of the French Revolution, she ould have had little idea that some

200 years later a waxwork museum bearing her name would – with its high-kitsch blend of celebrity likenesses and ghoulish dioramas – have become one of the country's most popular tourist attractions. At the adjacent Planetarium, you can see a hi-tech presentation on the wonders of the cosmos projected on to the ceiling of its famous dome. *Adm. Open 9.30am-5.30pm daily. Marylebone Road NW1, T: 0870 999 0046, www.madametussauds.com*

Museum of London ● 3G
The museum explores the development of the city over the past 2,500 years – from prehistoric camps to internet cafés. Look out for The Lord Mayor of London's ceremonial coach, which is still used in the Lord Mayor's Show every year (*see p.61*). The lower galleries are closed until 2010 for refurbishment. *Open 10am-6pm daily. London Wall EC2, T: 020 7001 9844, www.museumoflondon.org.uk*

Musical Museum ● 6A (off map)
The world's largest collection of self-playing musical instruments are housed in this new lottery-funded museum – everything from a tiny musical box to the 'Mighty Wurlitzer'. The fascinating Steam Museum is located nearby. *Adm. Open 11am-5.30pm Tue-Sun. 399 High Street, Brentford TW8, T: 020 8560 8108, www.musicalmuseum.co.uk*

National Gallery ● 4F/●
The country's premier art gallery where more than 2,000 chronologically arranged paintings – works by da Vinci, Rembrandt, Constable, Van Gogh, Monet and Picasso – trace the development of

Entrance to the Museum of London

see it

Find the Famous
Follow in the footsteps of the famous; look out for blue plaques that adorn the sides of houses to indicate that someone famous lived there. High-profile former residents of London include Virginia Woolf at 29 Fitzroy Square W1, Karl Marx at 28 Dean Street W1, Charles Dickens at 48 Doughty Street WC1, Oscar Wilde at 34 Tite Street SW3 and Nancy Astor (Britain's first female MP) at 4 St James Square SW1.
www.english-heritage.org.uk

western art from the 13th-20th century. *Open 10am-6pm Thu-Tue, 10am-9pm Wed. Trafalgar Square WC2, T: 020 7747 2885, www.nationalgallery.org.uk*

National Portrait Gallery ❷ 4F/❺
Spend hours browsing more than 10,000 portraits from Tudor kings and queens to JK Rowling. The first-floor gallery displays depictions of modern icons in a variety of different styles and mediums, with superb pictures of the Kinnocks and Blur's famous greatest hits album cover. Recognised portraits from the earlier centuries include Shakespeare and Elizabeth I on the second floor. *Open 10am-6pm Sat-Wed, 10am-9pm Thu-Fri. St Martin's Place WC2, T: 020 7312 2463, www.npg.org.uk*

Natural History Museum ❶ 5C
A colossal cathedral to nature whose main draw is the 26m- (85ft-) high diplodocus dinosaur skeleton. In addition to its two main sections, the Life Galleries (dinosaurs, mammals, birds) and the Earth Galleries (earthquakes, volcanoes, hurricanes), the museum boasts a shiny new

Darwin Centre (from September 2009), a lecture hall-cum-laboratory where you can take behind-the-scenes tours. The museum also has an excellent kids' programme and free backpacks for the under sevens. *Open 10am-5.50pm daily. Cromwell Road SW7, T: 020 7942 5000, www.nhm.ac.uk*

St James's Park ❷ 6D-7F
With its grand landscaping – the work of the great 17th-century French gardener André Le Nôtre – and elegant lake which provides a home to a range of wildfowl, including swans, geese and even pelicans, this may well be the

10

Cruising the Thames

There is a relaxing and oft-overlooked way of getting around this hectic city: City Cruises operates a hop-on, hop-off ferry service (ask for a Rover ticket) stopping at Westminster Pier, Waterloo Pier, Tower Pier and Greenwich Pier (*Daily, all year. T: 020 7740 0400, www.citycruises.com*). You can also take a leisurely cruise from Westminster Pier with Westminster Passenger Services upriver to Kew Gardens, Richmond and Hampton Court, south-west of the city centre (*Apr-Oct. T: 020 7930 2062, www.wpsa.co.uk*).

apital's most beautiful park. ordered by the royal residences of uckingham Palace (*see p.4*), St mes's Palace (where Prince Charles ves) and Clarence House (the ormer home of the Queen Mother),

it is a perfect spot to hire a deckchair and take a break from the bustle of London life. *Open 5am-12midnight daily. www.royalparks.gov.uk*

St Paul's Cathedral 1 3G

Sir Christopher Wren's masterpiece was completed in the early 18th century and its great plump dome still dominates the city skyline. The façade was recently restored for the building's 300th anniversary in 2008. There are 521 thigh-busting steps leading up to the topmost viewing gallery, from where you can enjoy great views out over the city. If the thought of climbing to the top leaves you puffed out, aim for the 259 steps that take you to the Whispering Gallery, where you can clearly hear the whispers from the other side of the gallery and the nave down below. *Adm. Open 8.30am-4pm Mon-Sat. St Paul's Churchyard EC4, T: 020 7236 4128, www.stpauls.co.uk*

Science Museum 1 5C

From steam engines to computers, spinning jennies to rockets – the museum provides a complete overview of technological innovation over the centuries. The opening of the Wellcome Wing, with its hi-tech displays and Imax cinema, as well as the Dana Centre where live science events are held, has helped to keep it on the cutting edge. Superb hands-on exhibits, such as building bridges,

St Paul's Cathedral

will keep the kids, from toddlers to teenagers, happy for hours. *Open 10am-6pm daily. Exhibition Road SW7, T: 020 7942 4000, www.sciencemuseum.org.uk*

Shakespeare's Globe ❶ 4G

This full-scale recreation of the Shakespearean theatre, built using traditional materials and methods, is very near the spot where the original Globe burnt down in 1613. Choose to watch a performance sitting on a wooden seat (bring or hire a cushion) or suffer as the average Elizabethan would have done and stand in the open-air yard in front of the stage (they sell plastic macs in the shop should it rain). There's also a multimedia exhibition of the theatre's history and there are guided tours of the theatre. *Adm. Open 9am-5pm May-Sep, 10am-5pm Oct-Apr, call well in advance for performance times. Bear Gardens, Bankside SE1, T: 020 7902 1500, www.shakespeares-globe.org*

Sherlock Holmes Museum ❶ 2C

Located at the fictional detective's well-known address, this museum to Sir Arthur Conan Doyle's most famous character faithfully resembles descriptions of the Victorian interior of the investigator's home, complete with deerstalker, pipe and slippers, as described by the author. Actors take up the roles of Sherlock Holmes, Dr Watson and Mrs Hudson. *Adm. Open 9.30am-6pm daily. 221b Baker Street NW1, T: 020 7935 8866, www.sherlock-holmes.co.uk*

All the world's a stage: Shakespeare's Globe

Somerset House ❷ 4H

Enjoy the architectural splendour of this grand mansion, built in the late 18th century to replace a derelict Tudor palace. Stroll through the shooting fountains in its courtyard with special shows every half hour, admire its grand river views and visit its prestigious collections: the Courtauld Gallery *(see p.5)* and the Hermitage Rooms. At Christmas, a temporary ice-skating rink is set up in the courtyard. *Free entry to courtyard and river terrace. Open 10am-6pm daily. Free tours 1st and 3rd Sat of the month. The Strand WC2, T: 020 7845 4600, www.somerset-house.org.uk*

South Bank & Bankside ❷ 5H-7H

Strolling along the south bank of the Thames is a pleasant way to spend a few hours, see some sights and feel part of London life. Starting from Westminster Pier pass the London Eye *(see p.8)*, until you reach the Royal Festival Hall and Southbank centre, where on Friday evenings you can catch a free, live jazz concert *(see box p.32)*. The waterside teems

...with life especially at the weekend, and there is a large daily second-hand book market held under Waterloo Bridge. Stop off at Gabriel's Wharf, a small, delightful complex of artisans' shops and riverside restaurants, before heading towards the landmark OXO tower, a former power station acquired by the OXO company, with its shops and restaurants (see p.39). For the more adventurous or energetic, carry on to the Tate Modern (see right), the Millennium Bridge and Shakespeare's Globe (see p.12) at Bankside. You could even walk all the way to London Bridge, passing Sir Francis Drake's 16th-century galleon The Golden Hind.
www.southbanklondon.com

Tate Britain ❶ 5E

Now that its mind-blowing modern art collection has moved to the Tate Modern (see right), the old Tate is free to concentrate on what it does best – showcasing British talent throughout the ages. All the great British names are here – Constable, Gainsborough, Hogarth, Epstein, Spencer, Stubbs, Hockney, Moore, Hepworth, Blake and Turner – in what is undoubtedly the country's greatest homage to a fantastic heritage of national art. *Open 10am-6pm daily. Millbank SW1, T: 020 7887 8000, www.tate.org.uk*

Tate Modern ❶ 4G

Lavished with praise on its opening, this former monolithic power station in Bankside is now firmly established as one of Europe's leading modern art galleries. With works by the

Former power station: Tate Modern

Tate à Tate
Take the catamaran, with a Damien Hirst designed livery, which shuttles between both Tate galleries (see below) with a stop at the London Eye (see p.8) every 40 minutes. Buy tickets from Tate galleries, phone or online.
T: 020 7887 8888,
www.tate.org.uk/tatetotate

likes of Picasso, Rothko and Pollock on permanent display, it also plays host to a succession of high-profile temporary exhibitions, and extra-large one-off displays in the vast, cathedral-like Turbine Hall. There are free activities for children to help engage them with the displays. Enjoy fantastic panoramic views of St Paul's (see p.11), the Thames and the Millennium Bridge from the fifth floor and the museum's Level Seven café. *Open 10am-6pm Sun-Thu, 10am-10pm Fri-Sat. Bankside SE1, T: 020 7887 8000, www.tate.org.uk*

Tower Bridge ❶ 4H

After Big Ben (see p.6), this great pinnacled bridge, finished in 1894, is perhaps the most photographed structure in all London. On the Tower Bridge Experience you can learn how its mighty decks are raised (when a large vessel comes upriver) and take a walk along one of the two covered walkways at the top of the bridge, which offer great views up and down the Thames. *Open 10am-6.30pm daily Apr-Sep, 9.30am-5pm daily Oct-Mar. Tower Hill EC3, T: 020 7403 3761, www.towerbridge.org.uk*

Kids having fun at Tower Bridge

Tower of London ❶ 4H

The Crown Jewels, including the sparkling Coronation Crown and Mace, are guarded by the resident Yeoman Warders, commonly known as the Beefeaters, also acting as guides – try to catch one of their informative tours. Constructed on the orders of William the Conqueror, the tower has stood guard over the city for nearly 1,000 years. It was used as a prison during the Middle Ages and its more illustrious captives included Anne Boleyn, the hapless second wife of Henry VIII, and the two princes allegedly murdered on the orders of Richard III. *Adm. Open 9am-5.30pm Tue-Sat, 10am-5.30pm Sun-Mon Mar-Oct, 9am-4.30pm Tue-Sat, 10am-4.30pm Sun-Mon Nov-Feb. Tower Hill EC3, T: 0844 482 7777, www.hrp.org.uk*

The Tower of London

Victoria & Albert Museum ❶ 5C

Large, rambling and somewhat confusingly laid out, the grand V&A South Kensington is nonetheless the city's finest collection of decorative arts. Its 11km (7 miles) of galleries hold a treasure trove of silverware, costumes, sculptures, paintings, ceramics and porcelain. Collections

Victoria and Albert Museum

...lude fashion from the 17th
...ntury to the present day including
...th-century designers such as Mary
...ant and Vivienne Westwood,
...ntemporary graphic arts, and
...dern-life ephemera from the
...phone through to the ipod.
...en 10am-5.45pm Sat-Thu,
...am-10pm Fri. Cromwell Road SW7,
...20 7942 2000, www.vam.ac.uk

...stminster Abbey ❶ 5E

...w a hot destination on the *Da*
...ci Code grand tour, this Gothic
...ey opposite the Houses of
...liament is a memorial to the
nation, filled with the tombs of the
country's greatest monarchs,
politicians, poets, scientists and
musicians. Look out for the
Coronation Chair, on which all but
one of Britain's monarchs have been
crowned since 1308. *Adm. Open
9.30am-4.30pm Mon-Sat. Dean's Yard
SW1, T: 020 7222 5152,
www.westminster-abbey.org*

Westminster Cathedral ❶ 5E

Built in Byzantine style, this ornate
Catholic church was completed in
the early 20th century, with a dome
and soaring belltower made of red
brick with white stripes. The nave is
the widest of any church in England
and you can see the High Altar from
all seats. Try to catch the sublime
Westminster Cathedral Choir who
sing daily Mass and Vespers, with
organ recitals every Sunday at
4.45pm. Not to be confused with
Westminster Abbey. *Open 7am-
7pm daily. Viewing Gallery open
9.30am-12.30pm & 1pm-5pm daily.
42 Francis Street SW1,
T: 020 7798 9055,
www.westminstercathedral.org.uk*

Altar inside Westminster Abbey

london places to shop

Boasting everything from antique markets where you can hunt for
bargains at the crack of dawn to world-famous department stores,
chic boutiques filled with high fashions to labyrinthine bookshops
and vast music emporiums, London is a city made for spending.
Indeed, the shopping bug has grown so strong in the capital that
many of its best shopping areas, such as Oxford Street (with four
tube stations along its length), Knightsbridge (home to Harrods and
Harvey Nichols) and Covent Garden (plus its surrounding streets full
of funky stores), as well as the markets at Camden Lock and
Portobello Road, have become tourist attractions in their own right.

buy it places to shop

Shopping Areas

Carnaby Street ❷ 3D

Once part of 1960s 'Swinging London' (see also King's Road, right), the area became run down and so has been beautifully redeveloped into a wide pedestrianised street with small independent clothes stores and bright, clean modern shops selling funky sports, surf and ski wear. Neighbouring Kingly Street has some lovely little shops and cafés; also take a peek at the stores in Kingly Court, a three-floor former timber warehouse with courtyard.
www.carnaby.co.uk

Camden Market

Hugely popular with students and tourists, several markets make up this bustling area in London's famous Camden Town. You'll find an eclectic collection of retro fashions, jewellery, antiques, posters and memorabilia, plus plenty of places to stop and eat.
www.camdenlock.net

Charing Cross Road ❷ 2F-4F/ ❻

The area for book browsing, where you'll find several of the big names – Blackwell, Borders, Foyles (see p.23), Waterstone's – surrounded by a cluster of secondhand book stores.

Covent Garden ❷ 3H/ ❻

The former fruit and veg market area (see p.5) is now a thriving centre of culture and commerce. Apple Market and Jubilee Market sell antiques, handicrafts, handmade jewellery, gems, clothes and souvenirs. Around the piazza, stock up on some of the high-street labels, or take a wander into the surrounding Floral Street, Neal Street, Monmouth Street and Seven Dials for funky little stores selling everything from tea, shoes and tarot cards, to unique, trendy clothes, organic food and cosmetics.
www.coventgardenlife.com

Jermyn Street ❷ 5D-4E

Lined with shops that seem to be inhabiting some sort of time warp, Jermyn Street is where the refined English gentleman can be found buying his tailored suits, collared shirts and Cuban cigars.

Shopping in Covent Garden Piazza

King's Road ❶ 6B-5D

The centre of 1960s 'Swinging London' is still going strong. Expect chic boutiques, smart restaurants, pavement cafés, exclusive antique shops and lots of well-groomed people parading up and down.

Knightsbridge ❶ 4C

The home of British haute couture, Knightsbridge is the shopping area of choice for fashion-conscious people with money to burn. Boasting the capital's two most well-to-do stores – Harrods (see p.

d Harvey Nichols *(see p.20)* – its
reets (particularly Brompton Road,
pane Street, Beauchamp Place) are
ed with designer-clothes stores.

ew & Old Bond Streets ② 2C-4D
he of the most exclusive shopping
eets in London, Bond Street is a
ecca for celeb clients seeking high-
hion designers: Chanel, Donna
ran, Versace, D&G, Gucci, Jimmy
oo; and jewellery: Cartier and
aff. It's also home to the auction
uses, Sotheby's and Phillips.

ford Street & Regent Street
3A-2F/2D-4E
r many people, these two great
ecting shopping streets are the
y essence of London, hence
 huge swarming crowds that
ngregate here every weekend.
ford Street is lined with
partment stores: M&S, John Lewis,
*ridges, Debenhams, big-name
ins and cheap and cheerful
uvenir stalls, while sweeping
jent Street is a touch more
gant, possessing graceful
hitecture and genteel choices:
erty's and Laura Ashley, mixed in

with state-of-the-art shops such as
the Apple Store.

Tottenham Court Road ② 1F-2F
In amongst a smattering of upmarket
interior design stores and high-street
shops, you can pick up a bargain in
one of the electronic and computer
goods retailers.

Westfield London ① off map at 3A
Opened in 2008, this luxury
shopping centre has 265 high street
and premium retailers – 16 making
their UK debut – and 50 restaurants,
you may want to make a day of it.
*Open 10am-9pm Mon-Wed,
10am-10pm Thu-Fri, 9am-9pm Sat,
12pm-6pm Sun. Ariel Way W12.
ukwestfield.com/london*

Department Stores

Fortnum & Mason ② 5E
Elegant and refined or stuffy and
old fashioned (depending on how
you look at things), Fortnum prides
itself on its status as a conveyor of
comestibles to the aristocracy. Its

justly famous tea hall is on the
ground floor *(see p.25). 181 Piccadilly
W1, T: 020 7734 8040,
www.fortnumandmason.co.uk*

Harrods ① 5C
A national institution, sometimes
subsumed beneath the gargantuan
personality of its owner, Mohamed
Al Fayed, Harrods is still London's

Harrods by night

pre-eminent department store. With a mighty 1.8 ha (4½ acres) of floor space, the shop stocks everything from fashion to pets, toys to sporting goods. Its magnificent 17-department food halls are one of the highlights as well as the Egyptian Hall on the Lower Ground and Ground floors and the Egyptian-themed escalators which run through the centre of the store. *87-135 Brompton Road SW1, T: 020 7730 1234, www.harrods.com*

Harvey Nichols ❶ 4C

'Harvey Nics' is Harrods' younger, groovier sibling. Smaller and with a narrower range of luxury goods, it is best known for its designer

Hunt Down a Bargain

Large-scale sales at the city's department stores (where reductions of 50% or greater are commonplace) take place twice a year in January and July. The most famous are held by Harrods (see p.19), when huge crowds descend on the store hunting for the ultimate bargain.

---

clothes and fabulous food hall. *109-125 Knightsbridge SW1, T: 020 7235 5000, www.harveynichols.com*

House of Fraser ❷ 2C

A mid-size department store specialising in mid-range fashions – Rive Gauche, Burberry, Jasper Conran and so on – at medium prices. Good for coats and cosmetics. *318 Oxford Street W1, T: 0845 602 1073, www.houseoffraser.co.uk*

John Lewis ❷ 2C

Don't go expecting high fashions; this is a no-nonsense kind of a place. It's particularly good for housewares,

haberdashery and ready-to-wear clothes. *Oxford Street W1, T: 020 7629 7711, www.johnlewis.cc*

Liberty ❷ 3D

Housed in a lovely Tudor-style building, Liberty has an artsy-crafts sort of vibe with very good fashion and furniture departments – its printed scarves find their way into million parcels come Christmas. *210-220 Regent Street W1, T: 020 7734 1234, www.liberty.co.uk*

Liberty at sale time

Portobello Road Market

Marks & Spencer ❷ 3B

M&S is a formidable British institution and still the place for ready-made meals and quality, affordable underwear as well as its own range of stylish women's clothes. **Main branch**: *458 Oxford Street W1, T: 020 7935 7954, www.marksandspencer.com*

Peter Jones ❶ 5D

Considering its location and typically Chelsea-Belgravia clientele, much of the merchandise at Peter Jones (part of the John Lewis group) is surprisingly affordable. Posh yet homey, it's good for linens and fabric. *Sloane Square SW1, T: 020 7730 3434, www.peterjones.co.uk*

Selfridges ❷ 3B

Selfridges is lively, vibrant, and somewhat maze-like. It is very big, with a huge range of goods on offer, and some excellent places to stop for a bite to eat. *400 Oxford Street W1, T: 0800 123 400, www.selfridges.co.uk*

Markets

Bermondsey Market ❶ 5H

This antiques market appears Brigadoon-like every Friday morning. Get up early – the bargains will be gone by 9am. *Open 4am-3pm Fri. Bermondsey Square SE1.*

Berwick Street Market ❷ 3E

Berwick Street Market is an excellent source of good quality fruit and veg, cheese, bread and spices, and has an old-fashioned feel to it. *Open 8am-6pm Mon-Sat. Berwick Street, Soho W1.*

Brick Lane Market ❶ 2H

Taste local life in this typical East End market selling cheap household goods, clothes and bits and pieces of tatty jewellery. *Open 8am-2pm Sun. Brick Lane E1.*

Borough Market ❶ 4G

Winner of a variety of awards, including NABMA Best Speciality Maket 2008 Award, this is a real foodies' market with a fabulous selection of meats, fish, vegetables, fruit, exotic cheeses, bread, coffee and spices. *Open 11am-5pm Thu,*

12pm-6pm Fri, 9am-4pm Sat.
Southwark Street SE1,
T: 020 7407 1002,
www.boroughmarket.org.uk

Columbia Road Flower Market
①off map at 1H

Start your Sunday morning in this lovely, vibrant flower market with stalls filled with colourful blooms, shrubs, bedding plants and, come December, Christmas trees and mistletoe. It's a trek by tube but worth the effort. *Open 8am-2pm Sun. Columbia Road E2, www.columbia-flower-market.freewebspace.com*

Columbia Road Flower Market

Greenwich Markets
①(Greenwich inset)

Greenwich (*see p.6*) is home to three excellent markets – an antiques market (off Greenwich High Road), a delightful covered craft market (College Approach), and a sprawling central market (Stockwell Street) selling clothes, books and furniture. *Open 11am-7pm Wed, 10am-5pm Thu-Fri, 10am-5.30pm Sat-Sun. www.greenwich-market.co.uk*

Petticoat Lane Market
①off map at 3H

A cheery, honest-to-goodness street market specialising in cheap fashion, knock-off goods, jewellery and second-hand tat. *Open 9am-2pm Sun-Fri. Middlesex Street E1*

Portobello Road Market **①3A**

Popular flea market and stores with everything from antiques and vintage clothes, to fruit and veg and household goods. **General Market** *Open 8am-6pm Fri-Wed, 8am-1pm Thu;* **Antique Market** *Open 5.30am-5pm Sat. Portobello Road, Notting Hill W10, T: 020 7229 8354, www.portobelloroad.co.uk*

Antiques

Antiquarius **①6C**

Over a hundred stalls selling a vast range of antiques, memorabilia and (for want of a better word) junk. *131-141 King's Road SW3, T: 020 7823 3900, www.antiquarius.co.uk*

Silver and antiques at the market

Art

ther Criteria ❶ 3D

amien Hirst's specialist store sells
blications, posters and prints from
tablished and emerging artists.
Hinde Street W1, T: 020 7935 5550,
ww.othercriteria.com

Bookshops

yles' ❷ 2F

yles' astonishingly eclectic layout
the stuff of legend. With copious
nounts of titles, it's famed for
cking the stuff other stores don't.
3-119 Charing Cross Road WC2,

nfords is famous for maps and guidebooks

T: 020 7437 5660, www.foyles.co.uk

Stanfords ❷ 3G

London's premier map and travel-
guide bookshop. 12-14 Long Acre
WC2, T: 020 7836 1321,
www.stanfords.co.uk

Waterstone's ❷ 4E

This branch is the largest bookshop
in Europe, with a fifth-floor café
and bar with views of the capital.
203-206 Piccadilly W1,
T: 0843 290 8549,
www.waterstones.co.uk

Cosmetics

Ormonde Jayne ❶ 5D

This glamorous perfumery has a
number of stores within London and
offers an innovative 'Perfume
Portrait' service, which helps to
guide customers towards their own
signature fragrance blend from 21
raw ingredients. 192 Pavillion Road
SW1, T: 020 7730 1381,
www.ormondejayne.com

The Porchester Spa ❶ 3B

For a more authentic and affordable

spa experience why not try the pools
and unfussy treatments, such as a
hot towel wrap, at the historic
Porchester Centre. The Porchester
Centre, Queensway W1, T: 020 7792
2919, www.better.org.uk

The Sanctuary ❷ 3G

Stop off for a bit of pampering after
a hard day's shopping frenzy, and
relax in a fluffy robe around the pool
or treat yourself to some of the
blissful products in the store.
12 Floral Street, Covent Garden WC2,
T: 020 770 3350,
www.thesanctuary.co.uk

Designer Fashion

Chloé **❶** 5D

Stella McCartney's ready-to-wear collection remains a popular choice for those wanting to follow the designer of the moment who recently dressed the British Olympians. *152-153 Sloane Street, T: 020 7823 5348, www.chloe.com*

Go Antiquing

London's thriving antiques scene attracts thousands of dealers, collectors and tourists every week. Try **Camden Passage** for a vibrant collection of shops offering antiques and bric-a-brac, hidden away down a cobblestoned back street in Islington; lively outdoor market stalls attract the crowds on Wednesdays and Saturdays. Or visit **Grays** off Oxford Street, home to over 200 dealers specialising in everything from ancient iconography to medieval jewellery and Matchbox cars.

Irregular Choice **❷** 3E

The place to go for quirky and eye-catching footwear. The store is choc full of founder-designer, Dan Sullivan's creations. *39 Carnaby Street W1, T: 020 7494 4811, www.irregularchoice.co.uk*

Jimmy Choo **❷** 4D

Shoe lovers can't miss a visit to one of London-based designer, Jimmy Choo's stores. *27 New Bond Street W1, T: 020 7493 5858, www.jimmychoo.com*

Matthew Williamson **❷** 4C

One of the latest celeb-designers, his modern, fresh, feminine clothes are renowned for bright colours and unique prints. *28 Bruton Street W1, T: 020 7629 6200, www.matthewwilliamson.com*

Paul Smith **❷** 3G

This very English designer owns a couple of stores in Covent Garden selling his trademark shirts and own-brand designer fragrances. *40-44 Floral Street WC2, T: 020 7379 7133, www.paulsmith.co.uk*

Discount

Browns Labels for Less **❷** 3C

Permanently low sale prices on designer labels, as well as discounted Browns Own fashions for men and women. *24-27 South Molton Street W1, T: 020 7514 001 www.brownsfashion.com*

Museum Shops

British Museum Store **❷** 1G

For unique gifts based on the museum's exhibits. *Great Court, British Museum, Great Russell Street WC1, T: 020 7637 1292, www.britishmuseum.co.uk*

London Transport Museum **❷** 3H

London gifts embossed with the Underground logo prove a popular souvenir – treat the kids to an Angel Station t-shirt. The shop also stocks one of the most comprehensive ranges of vintage transport posters around. *Covent Garden Piazza WC2, T: 020 7379 6344, www.ltmuseumshop.co*

Music

HMV ● 2E
Huge entertainment supermarket with vast stocks of videos, DVDs, CDs and computer games.
*150 Oxford Street W1,
T: 020 7631 3423, www.hmv.co.uk*

Rough Trade ● 3A & off map at 2H
This independent record shop has been successfully trading for over 30 years. *130 Talbot Road W11,
T: 020 7229 8541;
1 Brick Lane E1, T: 0207 392 7788,
www.roughtrade.com*

Parfumerie

Penhaligon's ● 4D
Perfumier to the Queen, this tiny store in the Burlington Arcade stocks a huge bouquet of its own fragrances and sweet-smelling soaps.
*16 Burlington Arcade W1,
T: 020 7629 1416,
www.penhaligons.com*

Sporting Goods

Rugby Store ● off map at 5A
The largest rugby store in England offers souvenirs, memorabilia and leisurewear.
*Twickenham Stadium, Rugby Road TW1, T: 0870 405 2003,
www.rfu.com/therugbystore*

Tea

Fortnum & Mason ● 5E
Tea, tea and more tea – this very British drink has more flavours than ice cream in the most famous tea hall of all (*see p.19*). *181 Piccadilly W1, T: 020 7734 8040,
www.fortnumandmason.co.uk*

Toys

Benjamin Pollock's Toy Shop ● 3G
Olde-Worlde toys and games: a delightful, cramped first-floor shop full of puppets, kaleidoscopes and intricate paper theatres.
*44 Covent Garden Market WC2,
T: 020 7379 7866,
www.pollocks-coventgarden.co.uk*

Hamleys ● 3D
The country's most famous toy store – and perhaps the most crowded (and noisy) place on earth – Hamleys boasts five floors of toys, board games, teddy bears and computer games. *188-196 Regent Street W1, T: 0870 333 2455,
www.hamleys.com*

Hamleys is child heaven

london entertainment

It's easy to be entertained in London. Every day, the city plays host to hundreds of shows, plays, concerts, films, recitals and comedy performances. Major sporting events such as the London Marathon, Oxford & Cambridge Boat Race, Wimbledon Tennis Championships and Premier League football matches take place throughout the year, as do themed film seasons at places like the BFI Southbank (not to mention numerous star-laden Leicester Square premieres). With an unrivalled theatrical heritage, thriving music scene, superb sporting facilities, state-of-the-art cinemas and world-class arts venues such as the Royal Opera House, Barbican and Southbank Centre, it's little wonder that the city acts as a magnet for the world's greatest entertainers and performers.

watch it entertainment

What's On

For entertainment listings, the weekly entertainment magazine *Time Out* is an invaluable source, as is the *Evening Standard's Metro Life* supplement (published Thursdays) as well as the *Guide*, free with the *Guardian's* Saturday edition. Visit London operates an information hotline:
T: 0870 156 6366.

You can also check out the following:
www.visitlondon.com
www.londontown.com
www.thisislondon.co.uk
www.timeout.com

Tickets

Buy tickets direct from the venue – box offices are open 10am-8pm, or:

Society of London Theatre Guide

Operates the *tkts* Booth on Leicester Square (*see box, right*) for discounted on-the-day theatre tickets. T: 020 7557 6700, *www.officiallondontheatre.co.uk*

Cheap Tickets

Fancy seeing a show, but don't want to pay through the nose? Head down to the *tkts* booth (**➋**4F/**➎**) on Leicester Square which sells half-price tickets for West End shows on a first-come, first-served basis. It's four tickets per person max and a £2.50 booking fee. *Open 10am-7pm Mon-Sat, 12pm-3pm Sun.*
www.officiallondontheatre.co.uk

Ticketline

T: 0870 444 5556,
www.ticketline.co.uk

Ticketmaster

T: 0870 534 4444,
www.ticketmaster.co.uk

Theatre

With more than 40 commercial theatres staging anything from experimental comedies to Shakespearean tragedies by way of all-singing, all-dancing long-running musical extravaganzas, London's West End theatre scene is justifiably one of the most famous and well respected in the world.

Top Shows

The Lion King **➋**3H/**➎**

Disney's superb story of Simba the lion with Elton John's excellent musical score and award-winning puppets and costumes.
Lyceum, 21 Wellington Street WC2,
T: 0870 243 9000,
www.thelionking.co.uk

Mamma Mia! **➋**4F/**➎**

Abba's fantastic feel-good music set around the story of a girl seekin her father's identity. *Prince of Wales Theatre, Coventry Street W1,*
T: 0870 850 0393,
www.mamma-mia.com

Les Misérables **➋**3F/**➎**

Based on Victor Hugo's novel this operatic marvel is more commonly known as 'Les Mis'. *Queen's Theatre 51 Shaftesbury Avenue W1,*
T: 0870 950 0930,
www.lesmis.com

⑤ THEATRELAND

1. Adelphi
2. Albery
3. Aldwych
4. Apollo
5. Arts
6. Cambridge
7. Coliseum
8. Comedy
9. Criterion
10. Dominion
11. Donmar W'hse
12. Duchess
13. Duke of York's
14. Fortune
15. Garrick
16. Gielgud
17. Her Majesty's
18. ICA
19. Lyceum
20. Lyric
21. New Ambassadors
22. New London
23. Novello
24. Palace
25. Peacock
26. Phoenix
27. Piccadilly
28. Playhouse
29. Prince Edward
30. Prince of Wales
31. Queen's
32. Royal Opera Hse
33. St Martin's
34. Savoy
35. Shaftesbury
36. Royal Drury Lane
37. Royal Haymarket
38. Vaudeville
39. Whitehall
40. Wyndham's

We Will Rock You ❶ 2F/❺

Join in Queen's foot-stomping rock anthems, scripted by Ben Elton. *Dominion Theatre, 268-269 Tottenham Court Road W1, T: 0870 169 0116, www.queenonline.com/wewillrockyou*

Wicked ❶ 5D

This prequel to the Wizard of Oz story is receiving rave reviews. *Apollo Victoria, Wilton Road SW1, T: 020 7834 6318, www.wickedthemusical.co.uk*

Theatre Venues

Hackney Empire ❶ off map at 1H

This grand old dame, dating back to 1901, offers a mix of cutting-edge theatre, opera, music and dance. *291 Mare Street E8, T: 020 8985 2424, www.hackneyempire.co.uk*

Menier Chocolate Factory ❶ 4G

Housed in a former chocolate factory, feast on award-winning theatre and delicious cuisine in the excellent restaurant. *53 Southwark Street SE1, T: 020 7907 7060, www.menierchocolatefactory.com*

National Theatre ❶ 4F

One of the country's great theatrical complexes, the state-sponsored National boasts three auditoriums: the Olivier, the Lyttelton and the Cottesloe, where you can see everything from big budget musicals to work by new playwrights. *South Bank SE1, T: 020 7452 3000, www.nt-online.org*

The Old Vic ❶ 4F

Since 2003, Kevin Spacey has been artistic director, and the presence of the great Hollywood actor undoubtedly draws in the crowds. Be sure to book early. *Waterloo Road SE1, T: 0870 060 6628, www.oldvictheatre.com*

Regent's Park Open Air Theatre ❶ 2D

Now that the Royal Shakespeare Company (RSC) has decamped from the Barbican, this is one of the best places to see the Bard's work performed. Start with a picnic in the park (*see p.60*) and then take your seat for a night of alfresco drama. *Regent's Park NW1, T: 0870 060 1811, www.openairtheatre.org*

Royal Court ❶ 5D

This prestigious venue is dedicated to encouraging and staging challenging new writing. Its two theatres are at the centre of London's culture of playwriting. *Sloane Square SW1, T: 020 7565 5000, www.royalcourttheatre.com*

Shakespeare's Globe ❶ 4G

Experience 'authentic' Shakespearean performances at this re-creation of the Elizabethan venue where the audiences heckle the actors. For more details, *see p.12*.

Outside the National Theatre

Music & Ballet

Barbican Centre ❶ 2G

[...] most universally derided as an ugly modernist eyesore, the Barbican compensates for any aesthetic deficiencies with the quality of its facilities, which include performance spaces, theatres and cinemas. It's home to the London Symphony Orchestra and hosts performances by the BBC Symphony Orchestra

The Royal Albert Hall

and City of London Symphonia. *Silk Street EC2, T: 020 7638 8891, www.barbican.org.uk*

Holland Park Theatre ❶ 4A

Watch the Royal Ballet dance under the stars or listen to the peacocks in the park (see p.60) trying to outdo the opera singers, with the ruins of Holland House as an exquisite backdrop. Open-air performances only run in the summer months and are extremely popular so book well in advance. *Holland Park W8, T: 0845 230 9769, www.operahollandpark.com*

London Coliseum ❷ 4G/❺

The home of the English National Opera aims to bring 'opera to the masses', with some ticket prices for midweek performances available for as little as £10. *St Martin's Lane WC2, T: 0845 145 0200, www.eno.org*

Royal Albert Hall ❶ 4B

This 19th-century barrel-shaped venue stages a high-profile series of classical concerts, the Proms (see p.61), from mid-July to mid-September, culminating in an evening in which patriots belt out 'Rule Britannia'. *Kensington Gore SW7, T: 020 7589 8212, www.royalalberthall.com*

The Royal Opera House

Royal Opera House ❷ 3H/❻

The home of the Royal Opera and Royal Ballet is one of the sparkling jewels in the capital's classical music crown. Free concerts and exhibitions are held in the Floral Hall. *Covent Garden WC2, T: 020 7304 4000, www.roh.org.uk*

Sadler's Wells ❶ 1F

Now refurbished, this is one of the best places to see contemporary dance productions. *Rosebery Avenue EC1, T: 0844 412 4300, www.sadlers-wells.com*

Southbank Centre ❷ 5H

This vast concrete monument to stark functionalism has undergone a massive renovation with new upmarket restaurants and shops attracting a lively crowd. It's a great place to hear classical music with three celebrated venues – the **Royal Festival Hall**, the **Queen Elizabeth Hall** and the **Purcell Room**. *South Bank SE1, T: 0871 663 2500, www.southbankcentre.co.uk*

> **Free Music**
> Relax over lunch with a free classical concert held at St. Martin-in-the-Fields church (❷ 4G) on Mon, Tue & Fri at 1pm. On Wednesday evenings at 8pm, catch a jazz performance in the crypt. *Adm.* T: 020 7766 1100, www.stmartin-in-the-fields.org

Wigmore Hall ❷ 2C

A small, well-respected Art Nouveau concert hall – with wonderful acoustics – which specialises in chamber music and solo pianist performances. *35 Wigmore Street W1, T: 020 7935 2141, www.wigmore-hall.org.uk*

Rock & Pop

Dingwalls ❶ 1D

Part of the vibrant Camden scene, Dingwalls puts on rock, pop and indie acts five days a week. On Fridays and Saturdays it transforms into the **Jongleurs** comedy club (see p.33). *Middle Yard, Camden Lock NW1, T: 020 7428 5929, www.dingwalls.com*

O2 Academy Brixton (off map)

Groovy, sweaty, all-standing venue popular with up-and-comers and big stars (Madonna and the Stones). The sloping floor allows great views, even from the back. *211 Stockwell Road, Brixton SW9, T: 08444 772000, www.o2academybrixton.co.uk*

The O2 ❶ (Greenwich inset)

London's premier entertainment venue, the O2 boasts perfect sight-lines, comfy seats and plenty of toilets. It stages big name bands and artists, such as The Mighty Boosh and Girls Aloud, plus top sports events and exhibitions. It takes just a matter of hours to convert the O2 arena from a concert venue to a world-class sporting arena. *North Greenwich, T: 020 8463 2000, www.theo2.co.uk*

Jazz

Jazz Café ❶ 1D

Owned by the Mean Fiddler Group, this restaurant venue showcases funk, soul and folk as well as traditional and modern jazz. *5 Parkway, Camden NW1, T: 020 7485 6834, www.jazzcafe.co.*

Pizza Express Jazz Club ❷ 2F

A Soho institution – live jazz is served up in the basement every night, but book a table in advance. *10 Dean Street W1, T: 020 7437 951 or 0845 602 7017 to book, www.pizzaexpresslive.com*

music with no pretensions

nnie Scott's ❷ 3F

e most famous jazz venue of them
– all the greats have played here.
leed, to get a slot at Ronnie
ott's is very much a rite of passage
any aspiring jazz performer.
okey and cool. *47 Frith Street W1,
20 7439 0747,
w.ronniescotts.co.uk*

Club ❷ 2E

the vanguard of the punk
olution in the late 1970s, these
s the 100 Club tends to focus on
eter, less angry fare – jazz, soul,
k etc. *100 Oxford Street W1, T: 020
6 0933,www.the100club.co.uk*

Comedy

Comedy Café ❶ 2H

This purpose-built comedy venue,
brightly decorated and always
crowded, provides a regular turnover
of new and established acts. There is
a late bar, reasonable food and
dancing as well as the standup. All
customers are required to dine.
*Open 7pm Wed-Sat. 66 Rivington
Street EC2, T: 020 7739 5706,
www.comedycafe.co.uk*

Comedy Store ❷ 4F

The granddaddy of all comedy venues,
the Store, which opened in the late

1970s, attracts all the top stars – Rik
Mayall, Dawn French and Robin
Williams. The Comedy Store Players
provide improvised hilarity on
Wednesdays and Sundays.
*Haymarket House,
1a Oxendon Street SW1,
T: 0844 847 1728,
www.thecomedystore.co.uk*

Jongleurs ❶ 1C

The Jongleurs Group run high-quality
comedy evenings at four separate
venues across London at Battersea,
Bow, Camden and Watford.
*T: 0844 844 0044,
www.jongleurs.com*

Cheery façade of the Comedy Café

Cinema

BFI London Imax Cinema ❶ 4F
3D-extravaganzas are projected onto the biggest screen in Britain at this state-of-the-art facility housed in a stunning cylindrical building near Waterloo Station. *1 Charlie Chaplin Walk, South Bank SE1, T: 0870 787 2525, www.bfi.org.uk/imax*

London Imax lights up at night

BFI Southbank ❶ 4F
With more than 2,000 films – made up of classics, British rarities, foreign work and archived TV – shown each year, the BFI offers the most diverse cinematic programme of any London venue. It's also the venue for the annual London Film Festival staged every November. *South Bank SE1, T: 020 7928 3232, www.bfi.org.uk*

Empire ❷ 4F
Leicester Square WC2, T: 08714 714 714, www.empirecinemas.co.uk

Odeon Leicester Square and Odeon West End ❷ 4F
Leicester Square WC2, T: 0871 22 44 007, www.odeon.co.uk

Prince Charles Cinema ❷ 4F
Shows a mixture of new releases, cult classics and art-house flicks and offers cheaper seats than the other Leicester Square-area cinemas. *Leicester Place WC2, T: 020 7494 3654, www.princecharlescinema.com*

Vue West End ❷ 4F
Leicester Square WC2, T: 08712 240 240, www.myvue.com

Night Clubs

Fabric ❶ 2G
Huge venue, considered to be one of the best clubs in London despite the lack of big-name DJs. *77a Charterhouse Street EC1, T: 020 7336 8898, www.fabriclondon.com*

Heaven ❷ 4G
Traditionally a gay club, now popular with everyone. *Under the Arches, Villiers Street WC2, T: 020 7930 2020, www.heaven-london.com*

matter at the O2 ❶ (Greenwich inset)
State-of-the-art sounds, DJs and projection displays await you at this three-storey club and music venue. *North Greenwich, T: 020 8463 2000, www.theo2.co.uk*

Ministry of Sound ❶ 5G
The super-famous Ministry attracts all the top DJs and releases multi-million-selling dance CDs. *103 Gaunt Street SE1, T: 0870 060 0010, www.ministryofsound.com*

pectator Sport

ricket

rd's ❶1C

ear Regent's Park and regarded by
any as the 'home of cricket'.
John's Wood NW8,
020 7432 1066, www.lords.org

e Oval ❶6F

nnington SW11, T: 020 7582 6660,
ww.surreycricket.com

otball

embley Stadium (off map)

ernational matches are played at
fantastic newly rebuilt and
designed Wembley Stadium which
ened in 2007. *Empire Way,
mbley, Middlesex,
)20 8795 9000,
w.wembleystadium.com*

gby Union

ickenham (off map)

land plays its home matches at
ckenham. Every year, England,
es, Scotland, Ireland, France and
y battle it out in Europe's top
by competition, Six Nations

tournament. *Rugby Road,
Twickenham, Middlesex,
T: 020 8831 6527, www.rfu.com*

Tennis

All England Lawn Tennis and Croquet Club (off map)

Wimbledon is home of strawberries
and cream, interminable rain delays
and long queues. Centre and No.1
Court tickets are allocated by public
ballot some six months prior.
Queuing on match day takes hours

Twickenham, the home of English Rugby

and only entitles you to access the
outer courts. Sometimes return
tickets are available from 2pm
onwards. *Church Road, Wimbledon
SW19, T: 020 8971 2473,
www.wimbledon.org*

Participation Sport

Ice Skating

The most picturesque is the
outdoor rink set up at Somerset
House, open over the Christmas
period (*see p.12*).

Broadgate Ice Rink ❶2H

*Broadgate Circle, Eldon Street EC2,
T: 020 7505 4068,
www.broadgateinfo.net*

Swimming

Serpentine Lido ❶4C

Sunbathe or dip in the outdoor pool
in central London. *Open 10am-6pm
daily Jun-Sep. Hyde Park,
T: 020 7706 3422
T: 020 7352 6985,
www.serpentinelido.com*

london places to eat and drink

Britain is fast gaining a reputation for its culinary skills and it's London, as always, that's leading the way. Thanks to unprecedented expansion in the 1980s and 90s, London now has a restaurant scene fit to rival any in the world, with something to suit every taste and budget. This growth has been helped by the city's great ethnic diversity which has bred a corresponding culinary variety, and by celebrity chefs who have opened a series of world-class restaurants in prime locations throughout the city. So, whatever your preference, be it for curry, noodles, sushi, pasta, steak or fish 'n' chips, you'll find the restaurant to suit you somewhere in the capital.

taste it places to eat and drink

Price Guide
Per person without drinks
£ = less than £15
££ = less than £40
£££ = more than £40

American

All Star Lanes £ ❶ off map at 2H
Bowling, American cuisine, loud music and cocktails offer a heady mix. Branches at Holborn and Bayswater too. *The Old Truman Brewery, 95 Brick Lane E1, T: 020 7426 9200, www.allstarlanes.co.uk*

Bluebird bar and restaurant

Joe Allen £-££ ❷ 3H
Upmarket diner serving transatlantic favourites such as eggs Benedict, steaks and fried chicken, and popular with West End actors. *13 Exeter Street WC2, T: 020 7836 0651, www.joeallenrestaurant.co.uk*

Argentinian

The Gaucho Grill ££ ❷ 4E
Specialises, as you'd expect, in big fat juicy steaks. *25 Swallow Street W1, T: 020 7734 4040.*
Branches: *89 Sloane Avenue SW3, T: 020 7584 9901; 125 Chancery Lane WC2, T: 020 7242 7727, www.gauchorestaurants.co.uk*

British

Boisdale ££ ❶ 5D
Serves traditional Scottish dishes – haggis, beer-battered fish, tatties and neeps, as well as carefully sourced premium-quality beef – and stocks more than 200 varieties of whisky – the best selection in London. *15 Eccleston Street SW1, T: 020 7730 6922;*

It's a Wine World
Acting as a sort of shrine to wine, Vinopolis ❶ 4G sits on the South Bank close to the Globe Theatre (*see p.12*). Take a tour through the wine regions of the world, sample a fine vintage in Wine Wharf, buy a bottle or two in the extensive gourmet shop and t complete your experience, eat in the celebrated Cantina Vinopolis. *Open Thu-Mon. Guided tours. No. 1 Bank End SE1. T: 020 7940 8333, www.vinopolis.co.uk*

anch: *Swedeland Court, 202
hopsgate EC2S, T: 020 7283 1763,
ww.boisdale.co.uk*

Modern British

01 at ANdAZ ££ ❶ 3H

ax at the floating wine and
ampagne bar before dining in the
gant Grade II-listed dining room
classic British dishes such as
ached and roasted grouse breast
slow-cooked venison in red wine
d port. This modern and chic hotel
s undergone a £9 million make-
er. *40 Liverpool Street EC2,
020 7961 1234,
ww.london.liverpoolstreet.andaz.com*

ebird ££-£££ ❶ 6C

s is one of the best of Terence
nran's mighty chain of London
stro-domes; the complex boasts
well-respected restaurant, a
umptious deli, a café and bar. *350
g's Road SW3, T: 020 7559 1000,
ww.bluebird-restaurant.com*

een ££-£££ ❶ 1G

nks to the accompanying TV
es, Jamie Oliver's 'charity'

restaurant, in which he trains
underprivileged kids to work in his
kitchen, is probably the city's best
known. The food is sumptuous, if
expensive, but all the profits go to
the charity. It's generally booked up
months in advance but they might
be able to squeeze you in at short
notice at the downstairs trattoria.
*15 Westland Place N1,
T: 0871 330 1515, www.fifteen.net*

Gordon Ramsay £££ ❶ 6C

The extremely well-heeled restaurant
of the famously temperamental chef
has been showered with praise, not
to mention Michelin stars. The food
is as modern and inventive as it gets.
Ramsay's ever-expanding restaurant
empire also includes eateries at
Claridge's and the Berkeley Hotel.
*68 Royal Hospital Road SW3,
T: 020 7352 4441,
www.gordonramsay.com*

The Ivy £££ ❷ 3F

The ultimate celeb hang-out
(where the paparazzi are seemingly
permanently encamped) is also an
exquisite restaurant (regularly voted
the capital's favourite) offering a

simple, beautifully crafted menu. You
need to book weeks in advance and
it helps if you're a TV star. *1 West
Street WC2, T: 020 7836 4751,
www.the-ivy.co.uk*

OXO Tower Restaurant £££ ❶ 4G

Set beneath the grand 1930s Art Deco
tower, one of the capital's great
landmarks stands alongside the
Thames, providing fantastic views out
over London and a good menu to
boot. The food is made up of a hotch-
potch of influences – Mediterranean,
French and British. *OXO Tower, Barge
House Street SE1, T: 020 7803 3888,
www.harveynichols.com*

Entrance to The Ivy

Quaglino's £££ ● 5E

Another trendy, star-studded eatery owned by the Conran empire, this serves expertly prepared cuisine in its beautiful dining room. *16 Bury Street SW1, T: 020 7930 6767. www.quaglinos.co.uk*

Rhodes Twenty Four £££ ● 3H

The celebrated TV chef's restaurant offers the twin delights of spectacular views (it's located on the 24th floor of one of the capital's highest buildings) and a menu dedicated to updating classic British cuisine – braised oxtail cottage pie, cockle and leek casserole, jam roly-poly and so on. Last orders 9pm, closed weekends. *Tower 42, Old Broad St EC2, T: 020 7877 7703, www.rhodes24.co.uk*

St Alban £££ ● 5F

The latest restaurant from former Ivy duo, Chris Corbin and Jeremy King. Cool, contemporary interiors, with Damien Hirst artworks on the wall, complement the delightful Mediterranean menu. *4-12 Lower Regent Street SW1, T: 020 7499 8558, www.stalban.net*

Skylon ££ ● 4F

With its sweeping views and excellent modern menu, this has become a favourite haunt of theatre- and concert-goers. *Level 3, Royal Festival Hall SE1, T: 020 7654 7800, www.southbankcentre.co.uk*

Chinese

There are Chinese restaurants on almost every London high street. For the best and most diverse Chinese cuisine, however, there's only really one place to go – Gerrard Street and Lisle Street (● 4F), two small roads just to the north of Leicester Square which together are at the heart of London's exotic Chinatown district.

Chuen Cheng Ku ££ ● 4F

This cavernous restaurant boasts the largest menu in Chinatown, which considering the competition, is quite some claim. The *dim sum* (Chinese dumplings) are particularly excellent

Did You Know?
That the OXO Tower's distinctive design was created to circumvent the strict anti-advertising laws in place in the 1930s?

...nd are served from trolleys from ...nchtime onwards, along with an ...ndless supply of green tea. *7 Wardour Street W1, 020 7437 1398, www.chuenchengku.co.uk*

Fish 'n' Chips

...his great British dish has undergone ...omething of a post-modern ...-evaluation of late and the number ...f upmarket fish and chip restaurants ...as increased dramatically in London ...uring recent years.

...vebait ££ ❶ 4G

...ith decor as fresh and pure as the ...ay's catch, it's difficult to go wrong ...ere. They serve everything from ...assic fish and chips to more ...dventurous fare – crab and prawn ...aguine perhaps. Great seafood ...atters. They also do a special ...ildren's menu. *43 The Cut SE1, 020 7928 7211, www.livebaitrestaurants.co.uk*

...ck & Sole Plaice £ ❷ 2G

...tablished in 1871, this is London's ...dest fish and chip shop and one of

the best. It serves all the traditional staples – cod, rock, haddock and plaice – with particularly good chips. Book at the weekends. Bring your own wine. *47 Endell Street WC2, T: 020 7836 3785.*

French

Le Bel Canto ££-£££ ❶ 3H

This restaurant concept brought over from Paris combines two of life's pleasures – food and opera. Singing waiters serve delightful specials of duck leg confit and baked camembert with balsamic syrup. Fixed-price menus. *Mark Lane EC3, T: 020 7444 0004, www.lebelcanto.co.uk*

L'Escargot £££ ❷ 3F

This bastion of garlic (owned by chef Marco Pierre White) has been feeding the denizens of London with tasty Gallic fare (including, the eponymous snails) for decades now. Upstairs in the Picasso Room you will find a decent-value set-lunch menu. *48 Greek Street W1, T: 020 7437 6828, www.lescargotrestaurant.co.uk*

Elevated Eating
Gaze at the London skyline in the sixth-floor Café on Level 7 at the Tate Modern (*see p.13*), the Studio Lounge at Waterstone's in Piccadilly (*see p.23*), the Fifth Floor restaurant at Harvey Nichols (*see p.20*), the Skylon at the Southbank (*see p.40*), Rhodes Twenty Four on the 24th floor of Tower 42 (*see p.40*) and, if you can afford it, the OXO Tower Restaurant (*see p.39*), a magical night-time dining experience. If your budget is tight, there's a free viewing platform next door to the OXO Tower Restaurant.

Galvin Bistrot de Luxe ££–£££ ❶ 3D

Enjoy a modern classic cuisine – from sautéed veal kidneys to roast veal brains – served in a classy, club-like setting. Voted French Restaurant of the Year in 2008. Set menus are good value. *66 Baker Street W1, T: 020 7935 4007, www.galvinrestaurants.com*

Indian

Curry has been named the nation's favourite dish. London boasts plenty of first-rate establishments in which to sample India's culinary delights.

Cinnamon Club £££ ❶ 5E

Occupying the grand open spaces of the former Westminster Library, the extremely well-to-do Cinnamon Club comes across as a mix between a gentlemen's club, a French deli and a (very) upmarket curry house, and is very popular with politicians and media types. There's a nice quiet bar beneath the main restaurant. *30-32 Great Smith Street SW1, T: 020 7222 2555, www.cinnamonclub.com*

Tamarind ££ ❷ 5C

This Michelin-starred popular restaurant offers what could perhaps be described as modern Indian, where the emphasis is on the presentation and re-interpretation of regional dishes to give them a distinctive style. *20 Queen Street W1, T: 020 7629 3561, www.tamarindrestaurant.com*

Veeraswamy ££–£££ ❷ 4E

One of central London's best curry houses has just been transformed into a luxuriously chic spot to unwind after a hard day's shopping. *99 Regent Street, T: 020 7734 1401, www.veeraswamy.com*

Famous façade of L'Escargot

Italian

Frankie's Sportsbar and Grill £ ❶ 6B off map

New to Chelsea Football Club, the latest Italian diner from jockey Frankie Dettori and chef Marco Pierre White serves pizza, pasta and burgers as well as salads and fish in a family-friendly environment. *Stamford Bridge SW6, T: 020 7957 8298, www.frankiesitalianbarandgrill.com*

Japanese

Nobu £££ ❷ 6B

As trendy as they come, this hybrid Japanese-American affair usually gathers together a smattering of celebrities come the weekend. Expect excellent cuisine and stark modern decor. Booking essential. *Metropolitan Hotel, 19 Old Park Lane W1, T: 020 7447 4747. www.noburestaurants.com*

Wagamama £ ❷ 3G, ❷ 1G, ❷ 3H

Diners eat fast food Japanese-style, with fresh noodle and rice dishes, a

The dining room at Veeraswamy

...ng shared tables. No booking required. **Branches:** *10a Lexington ...eet W1, T: 020 7292 0990; ...avistock Street WC2, ...020 7836 3330; 4a Streatham ...eet, T: 020 7323 9223; ...1a Wigmore Street W1, ...020 7409 0111; 14a Irving Street ...2, T: 020 7839 2323; Royal ...tival Hall SE, T: 020 7021 0877, ...w.wagamama.com*

...! Sushi £ ❷ 2F, ❸ 3E, ❶ 4C, ...3B, ❶ 4H

...ect sushi from a conveyor belt and ...served by the robotic drinks ...ter. **Branches:** *52 Poland Street ..., T: 020 7287 0443; 19 Rupert*

Street W1 T: 020 7434 2724: Harvey Nichols (see p.20); Paddington Station; 95 Farringdon Road EC1, T: 020 7841 0785; County Hall, Belvedere Road SE1, T: 020 7928 8871, www.yosushi.com

Moroccan

Momo ££ ❷ 4D

One of the best Middle Eastern restaurants in the city. All the couscous and tajines you can eat at this upmarket, spectacularly trendy Moroccan restaurant with authentic lanterns, cushions and brass tables. Listen to the resident DJs (you can even buy their CDs) in the bar, or enjoy pastries in the tearoom. *25 Heddon Street W1, T: 020 7434 4040, www.momoresto.com*

Catering for Kids

Many restaurants now go out of their way to welcome families, with funpacks and games for the kids and well-thought-out children's menus. Some even go so far as to lay on entertainment at weekends in the

shape of magicians or clowns. All branches of **TGI Friday's**, **Café Rouge**, **Maxwell's** and **Smollensky's** are particularly family friendly, as is the **Rainforest Café** (❷ 4E) where you get to eat your burgers and fries in a replica jungle setting while animatronic creatures chatter away in the background. It gets very busy at weekends, so pre-booking using the priority seating system is recommended. *20 Shaftesbury Avenue W1, T: 020 7434 3111, www.therainforestcafe.co.uk*

Modern eating at Yo! Sushi

Vegetarian Restaurants

Most menus have meat-free options, or try one of the veggie cafés below:

Food for Thought ❸3G
31 Neal Street WC2,
T: 020 7836 0239.

Mildreds ❷3E
45 Lexington Street W1,
T: 020 7494 1634, www.mildreds.co.uk

The Place Below ❶3G
Delicious soups and hot dishes in a crypt and opens Mon-Fri 7.30am-3.30pm. *St-Mary-le-Bow Church EC2, T: 020 7329 0789, www.theplacebelow.co.uk*

Vegetarian dishes to tempt you

Cafés

Bar Italia £ ❷3F
Cheery Soho café-bar open 24 hours a day from Monday to Saturday and on Sunday from 7am-4am. Great if you're feeling rather peckish at 3am. *22 Frith Street W1, T: 020 7437 4520, www.baritaliasoho.co.uk*

Brick Lane Bagel Bake £ ❶2H
Open 24 hours a day, this serves the best bagels in London. The salmon-and-cream cheese variety is particularly recommended. *159 Brick Lane E1, T: 020 7729 0616.*

Café in the Crypt £ ❷4G
Spooky subterranean café housed in the crypt of St Martin-in-the-Fields Church. It has a jolly atmosphere, despite its dungeon-esque locale, and the menu features lots of vegetarian choices. *St Martin-in-the-Fields Church, Duncannon Street WC2, T: 020 7766 1158, www2.stmartin-in-the-fields.org*

Franx Snack Bar £ ❷2G
Cheery 'greasy spoon' for a proper full English breakfast – eggs, bacon,

Early morning at Bar Italia

sausages, tomatoes and a fried slice. *192 Shaftesbury Avenue WC2, T: 020 7836 7989.*

ICA Café £ ❷5F
This arts-centre café is reasonably priced, stays open late (1am) but gets very crowded. *12 Carlton House Terrace, The Mall SW1, T: 020 7930 8619, www.ica.org.uk*

Patisserie Valerie £ ❷3F
The famous cafés stock a wonderful array of treats. **Branches:** *44 Old*

ompton Street W1, T: 020 7437 3466;
05 Marylebone High Street W1,
020 7935 6240;
5 Bedford Street WC2,
020 7379 6428;
7 Brushfield Street E1,
020 7247 4906,
ww.patisserie-valerie.co.uk

onti's Espresso £ ❷ 3G
rving an extensive range of Italian
ick bites, the food is good and the
mosphere lively. *4 The Piazza, Covent
rden WC2, T: 020 7836 0272.*

sserts at Patisserie Valerie

fternoon Tea

e following hotels and
ablishments offer afternoon or
gh' tea – which should usually

Pie and Mash
For a true taste of London,
eschew the fancy eateries and
head to south and east
London, homes of the pie and
mash shop. The menu is
simple: pies (steak or eel, or
sometimes a veggie option),
served with mash and a
parsley sauce called 'liquor'.
Try the following:
Goddard's, *Greenwich
Church Street SE10.*
G. Kelly's, *414 Bethnal
Green Road E2.*
F. Cooke's, *Hoxton Street N1.*
G. Kelly, *600 Roman Road E3.*
Manze's, *87 Tower Bridge
Road SE1.*

involve delicate sandwiches, scones,
cakes, clotted cream and strawberry
jam – served in opulent surroundings
for around £20 per head in the late
afternoon. A jacket and tie are
essential dress for the men and
it's advisable to book well in advance
– weeks in the case of the ever-
popular Ritz.

Brown's Hotel ££ ❷ 4D
*30 Albemarle Street W1,
T: 020 7493 6020,
www.brownshotel.com*

Claridge's ££ ❷ 3C
*Brook Street W1, T: 020 7629 8860,
www.claridges.co.uk*

Fortnum & Mason
Fountain Restaurant ££ ❷ 5E
181 Piccadilly W1, T: 020 7734 8040.

The Ritz ££ ❷ 5D
*150 Piccadilly W1, T: 020 7300 2345,
www.theritzlondon.com*

Savoy ££ ❷ 4H
*The Strand WC2, T: 020 7836 4343,
www.savoy-group.co.uk*

The Ritz at Christmas time

Pubs & Bars

Nights out in Britain are bound to include a trip to the pub; London is no exception. Nowadays there are three categories of drinking establishment: the traditional pub, cosy, friendly and probably serving ale; the chain pub, large, garish and lager-dominated; and the bar, trendy, sophisticated, noisy and keen on cocktails and wine.

While most pub-goers opt for cold fizzy lager, it's worth trying a sup of ale: darker, tastier and bitter. Recent changes to the law mean pubs can stay open 24 hours if they choose.

The Coal Hole

The Anchor ● 4G
With an outdoor terrace overlooking the river, this ancient pub provides an ideal spot to wind down after watching a performance at the Globe (see p.12). It was supposedly the location from where Samuel Pepys watched the Fire of London, before the pub itself burned down. *34 Park Street, Bankside SE1, T: 020 7407 1577.*

Cantaloupe ● 3E
Lively, fun and often extremely crowded modern bar. One of the places to be seen. *35-42 Charlotte Street EC2, T: 020 7729 5566, www.cantaloupe.co.uk*

Coach and Horses ● 3F
This pub is small and creaky but undeniably very, very London with cheap pints and sandwiches. *29 Greek Street W1, T: 020 7437 5920, www.normanscoachandhorses.com*

The Coal Hole ● 4H
Where Gilbert and Sullivan used to get together to discuss their latest productions, the Coal Hole attracts its fair share of thespians. It's on three levels and gets very crowded. *91 The Strand, T: 020 7379 9883.*

George Inn ● 4H
Such is the historic importance of this rambling 17th-century coaching inn – it stands near the site of the Tabard Inn, where Chaucer's pilgrims gathered to tell their tales – that it has been bought by the National Trust. *77 Borough High Street SE1, T: 020 7407 2056.*

Gordon's Wine Bar ● 5G
Hugely popular subterranean wine bar. Descending the stairs, it feels like entering a secret society; once inside it is relaxed but busy. *47 Villiers Street WC2, T: 020 7930 1408, www.gordonswinebar.com*

Name that Pub
Many of the names of traditional pubs – Lamb and Flag, Hoop and Grapes – were specially devised so as to be easy to represent pictorially on the pub sign, thus allowing illiterate drinkers to find the right hostelry.

op and Grapes ❶ 3H
is charming little pub is housed
one of the oldest buildings in the
ɔital (c.1500) and was one of the
v to escape the Fire of London.
Aldgate High Street EC3,
020 7481 4583.

mb and Flag ❷ 3G
cked up an alleyway near Covent
rden, this age-old pub
ipposedly one of the oldest in
ndon) is always packed with
ɔple. 33 Rose Street WC2,
020 7497 9504.

◦ Lamb and Flag

Market Porter ❶ 4G
A real ale pub; this is the place to
come if you fancy a convivial pint at
6am. It opens its doors early for the
benefit of the traders at nearby
Borough Market. It also featured in
movies including *Harry Potter and the
Prisoner of Azkaban* and *Mission
Impossible*. 9 Stoney Street SE1,
T: 020 7407 2495,
www.markettaverns.co.uk

Mash ❷ 2D
One of the better modern bars,
Mash has a style all its own. It can
get very crowded at the weekend.
19-21 Great Portland Street W1,
T: 020 7637 5555.

Pitcher & Piano ❷ 4G
Extremely popular Trafalgar Square
branch of the now ubiquitous chain.
40-42 William IV Street WC2,
T: 020 7240 6180,
www.pitcherandpiano.com

Ye Olde Cheshire Cheese ❶ 3F
This lively pub-cum-chop house first
opened for business back in the
1670s and can count Dr Johnson,
Dickens and Mark Twain among its

The Pitcher & Piano

former patrons. 145 Fleet Street EC4,
T: 020 7353 6170.

Sherlock Holmes ❷ 5G
Filled with artefacts and a replica of
the famous detective's study.
10 Northumberland Street WC2,
T: 020 7930 2644.

Vertigo42 ❶ 3H
Book in advance to enjoy a drink
(and the views) looking over London
from the 42nd floor of Tower 42.
A snack and seafood bar, it has room
for just 70 people. *Tower 42, 25 Old
Broad St EC2*, T: 020 7877 7842,
www.vertigo42.co.uk

london practical information

From a tiny settlement on the banks of the River Thames, London has grown over the course of the last 2,000 years into one of the largest cities in the world, a vast metropolis of more than 2,500km^2 (1,000 square miles) that provides a home to more than seven million people. Despite its size, there's no reason to feel daunted at the prospect of visiting London. Most of its main tourist attractions are actually located in or around central London, which can be easily navigated on foot. What follows will hopefully help you to get to grips with the finer details of London living – getting there, the transport system, currency and so on.

know it practical information

Tourist Information

Visit London
Tourist information offices are found in Victoria, Liverpool Street and Euston Stations, and at Heathrow Airport.
T: 08701 566 366,
www.visitlondon.com

Visit Britain ❷ 5E
Provides maps, a countrywide hotel booking service and sells the London Pass (see below).
1 Regent Street W1,
www.visitbritain.com

London Pass
The London Pass gives free entry to 55 of London's attractions, commission-free currency exchange, free internet access and discounts at restaurants. It costs:
1 day – adult £39, child £25;
2 days – adult £52, child £38;
3 days – adult £63, child £44;
6 days – adult £86, child £60.
www.londonpass.com

Arriving by Air

As befits a city of its size and status, London is served by five airports, but you're most likely to touch down at one of the two largest: Heathrow and Gatwick. The national carrier is British Airways: T: 0844 493 0777, www.britishairways.com

Heathrow

Heathrow, the busiest airport in the world, is located 24km (15 miles) west of London. There are several options for travelling into central London.

Airbus Heathrow Shuttle

Shuttle buses run every 30 minutes to stops in the city centre from 7.15am-11.30pm. Cost £4 single, £8 return. Under 15s travel free.
T: 08705 757 747,
www.nationalexpress.com

Heathrow Express ❶3B

Trains run every 15 minutes between the airport and Paddington Station, which connects to the tube. The journey takes 15 minutes and costs £16.50. T: 0845 600 1515, www.heathrowexpress.com

Check-in at Heathrow

Taxi

The most comfortable, convenient and most expensive option for getting into town. A black taxi from Heathrow to central London will cost in the region of £30-35 (more after 8pm). Taxi ranks are outside of the arrivals halls.
Radio Taxis: T: 020 7272 0272.

Underground (Tube) ❹

The Piccadilly Line connects Heathrow with central London between 5am and 12 midnight daily. The journey takes between 40 minutes and over an hour. A single adult ticket costs £4. It's not recommended in rush hours when the carriages become overcrowded.
www.tfl.gov.uk

...twick

...don's second largest airport is
...km (28 miles) south of central
...don. **Airport Enquiries:**
...870 000 2468.

...following options exist for
...velling into London:

...wick Express ❶ 5D

...ns run every 15 minutes from
...0am-12.30am daily direct to
...toria Station, and then every half
...hour through the night (single
...5, return £27). The journey takes
... over half an hour. A slow service
...ps at Croydon and Clapham
...ction. T: 0845 850 1530,
...w.gatwickexpress.co.uk

...wick Express at Victoria

National Express

Operates between 3.30am-11.30pm. A
single ticket costs £7, a return £12.50.
The journey to Victoria can take up to
two hours. T: 08705 757 747,
www.nationalexpress.com

Taxi

A black cab to London costs about
£50 to £60 and takes over an hour.

Smaller Airports

London City

6km (4 miles) east of the city.
A shuttle bus runs to Liverpool Street
Station. T: 020 7646 0088,
www.londoncityairport.com

Luton

51.5km (32 miles) north of London
and linked by direct train to Victoria
Station (one hour/£12.40).
T: 01582 405 100,
www.london-luton.co.uk

Stansted

56km (34 miles) from central
London. The Stansted Express links
with Liverpool Street Station.
T: 0845 600 7245,
www.stanstedexpress.co.uk

Arriving by Land

By Coach ❶ 5D

Victoria Coach Station services the
UK and Europe. It's a short walk to
Victoria Station, from where you can
catch trains and tubes. *52 Grosvenor
Gardens SW1, T: 08705 757 747,
www.nationalexpress.com*

By Eurostar ❶ 1F

Super-speedy Eurostar trains bring
continental visitors from Paris and
Brussels through the Channel Tunnel
to St Pancras International. The full
journey from Paris takes around two
hours 35 minutes (less from Brussels),
of which 25 minutes is spent in the
tunnel itself. St Pancras links to the
underground and has a taxi rank.

Eurostar at St Pancras International

St Pancras International NW1,
T: 08705 186 186, www.eurostar.com

By Train

There are direct rail services to London from all Britain's major cities. **Information:** T: 08457 48 49 50, www.nationalrail.co.uk

Getting Around

London Transport Enquiries
T: 020 7222 1234,
www.tfl.gov.uk

Travel Cards

Travel and Oyster Pre Pay cards permit unlimited travel on London's buses, tubes and trains. A one-day **travelcard** covering zones 1-2 (most of the sights are here) costs adults £6.30, and children £3.40 Mon-Fri. An adult off-peak travelcard can be bought after 9.30am and on Saturdays and Sundays for £5.30. Three-day cards are also available. Alternatively you can purchase an **Oyster Card** (for a refundable £3 deposit) and top it up as you go at stations and online; individual fare

Traditional London bus

prices then work out cheaper than standard ones.

Buses ❸

Bus routes cover much of central London but congestion problems make them less reliable than the tube during peak hours. They are useful for sightseeing and good value. Buy a ticket before you board from a ticket machine or newsagent. Day services run from 5am-12 midnight. Then nightbuses take over, most departing from Trafalgar Square (❷5F).

Cars

If you want to explore the city by car, you have to pay for the privilege:

a congestion charge of £8 per day (or £10 if you pay the following day), Monday-Friday from 7am-6pm is in effect from Grand Union Canal in North Kensington down to Holland Park along Chelsea Embankment, Elephant & Castle in the south, Tower Bridge in the east to King's Cross in the north. Entry points to the zone are marked with a giant red C on the road. Failure to pay will result in a £50 or £100 fine. The charge can be paid up by phone, online or at certain selected shops.
T: 0845 900 1234,
www.cclondon.com

Taxis

Black Taxis

London's iconic black cabs are not cheap but they are reliable – potential taxi drivers must commit every London street to memory before they qualify for their badge, which can take two years. Because each journey is metered, you know exactly what you owe. A taxi whose orange 'For Hire' sign is lit up can be hailed on the street.

black taxi

Minicabs

Minicabs are cheaper than black cabs, but drivers don't have to pass tests so their local knowledge may be scant. Most minicabs don't have meters so agree a price beforehand.

Underground/Tube  ❹

The underground railway network ('tube') is the quickest way of getting around London. With 12 colour-coded interconnecting lines traversing the city, you're always close to a tube station. The service is 5am-12 midnight daily.

Docklands Light Railway

In the Docklands and South East London, the tube is augmented by the DLR, a driverless overground monorail that joins up with the underground at Bank and Tower Hill.

Banks & Money

Banks and Bureaux de Change

The banks all operate cash dispensers for 24-hour withdrawal with Maestro symbol and credit cards. Each bank operates a bureau de change, with more found at airports and stations.

Currency

Britain's currency is the pound (£), divided into 100 pence (p). There are eight coin denominations: 1p, 2p, 5p, 10p, 20p, 50p, £1 and £2, and four notes: £5, £10, £20, £50.

An underground sign

Debit and Credit Cards

The majority of shops, restaurants and services accept all major credit cards and Maestro symbol cards, although you must know your PIN.

Climate

London is not always cold and foggy. The winters are cold; temperatures drop below zero, but conditions are damp rather than icy. Summer has plenty of sunny days as well as rainy ones. Average temperatures in Jul-Aug are 22°C (71.5°F), dropping to 7°C (44°F) during Dec-Jan.

Disabled Access

Visit London provides a wide range of information on access in London. *www.visitlondon.com/maps/accessibility*

Embassies

Australian High Commission ❶ 3F
Australia House WC2,
T: 020 7379 4334,
www.australia.org.uk

Canadian High Commission ❷ 4C
1 Grosvenor Square W1,
T: 020 7258 6600,
www.canada.org.uk

Irish Embassy ❷ 7C
17 Grosvenor Place SW1,
T: 020 7235 2171,
www.embassyofireland.co.uk

US Embassy ❷ 4B
24 Grosvenor Square W1,
T: 020 7499 9000,
www.usembassy.org.uk

Emergencies

The following hospitals have Accident and Emergency departments should you require:

Chelsea & Westminster ❶ 6B
369 Fulham Road SW10,
T: 020 8746 8000,
www.chelwest.nhs.uk

Guy's and St Thomas' ❶ 4H
Great Maze Pond SE1,
T: 020 7188 7188,
www.guysandstthomas.nhs.uk

Ambulance, fire and police: *T: 999.*

A London ambulance

Lost Property

**Transport for London
Lost Property Office** ❶ 2D
Open 8.30am till 4pm, Mon-Fri.
200 Baker Street NW1,
T: 0845 330 9882, www.tfl.gov.uk

Opening Hours

Banks are typically open 9.30am-5pm Mon-Fri, 9am-11.30pm Sat.

Shops usually open from 9.30am till 6 or 7pm Mon-Fri (some till 9pm Thu), 9am-5pm Sat, 11am-5pm Sun.

Pharmacies

Zafash ❶ 6B
London's only 24-hour chemist.
233 Old Brompton Road SW5,
T: 020 7373 2798.

Post Offices

Main Post Office ❷ 4G
Branches usually open Mon-Fri 9am-5.30pm, Sat 9am-1pm. Newsagent also sell stamps. It costs 36p up to 100g to send a letter first class in Britain, 48p surface mail and 50p airmail to send mail internationally.
Main Branch: *Open 8am-8pm daily,*
24-28 William IV Street WC2,
T: 0845 722 3344,
www.royalmail.com

Public Holidays

Banks close on the following days:

New Year's Day *1st Jan*
Good Friday *Mar-Apr (variable)*
Easter Monday *Mar-Apr (variable)*
May Day *First Mon May*
Spring Bank Holiday *Last Mon May*

…mmer Bank Holiday *Last Mon Aug*
…ristmas Day *25th Dec*
…xing Day *26th Dec*

…elephones

…blic phones take coins or
…onecards, available from
…wsagents and post offices.
…me booths accept credit cards.

…ephone box

Post box

…rectory Enquiries
…118 500,
…w.directoryenquiries.co.uk

…ours

…TG Blue Badge Guides
…pert guides. *T: 020 7780 4060,*
…w.touristguides.org.uk

Big Bus Company
Double-decker bus tours, starting
at Marble Arch. *T: 020 7233 9533,*
www.bigbustours.com

City Cruises
Westminster or Waterloo downriver
to Greenwich. *T: 020 7740 0400,*
www.citycruises.com

Jack the Ripper Walks
Two-hour walks around the alleys,
passages and streets of East London.
T: 020 8530 8443,
rippertour@aol.com
www.rippertour.com

London Bicycle Tour Company
T: 020 7928 6838,
www.londonbicycle.com

London Duck Tours
The amphibious vehicle tours the
roads and then drives into the river.
T: 020 7928 3132,
www.londonducktours.co.uk

London Waterbus Company
Canal trips *(see box p.9)* from
Camden Lock to Little Venice.
Apr-Sep. T: 020 7482 2660,
www.londonwaterbus.com

Original London Walks
Themed walks: 'Apparitions,
Alleyways and Ale', 'Princess Diana's
London' etc. *T: 020 7624 3978,*
www.walks.com

Thames River Boats
Trips from Westminster to Hampton
Court and Kew Gardens *(see box
p.11)*. Dinner cruises available.
Apr-Oct. T: 020 7930 2062,
www.wpsa.co.uk

Internet Access

Net House Internet Café ❶ 2C
Open daily. *138 Marylebone
Road NW1, T: 020 7224 7008*

easyEverything ❶ 5D
24-seven web access. Nine
central branches. *9-13 Wilton
Road SW1, T: 020 7233 8456,*
www.easyinternetcafe.com

Portobello Gold ❶ 3A
Open daily. *95-97 Portobello
Road W10, T: 020 7460 4910,*
www.portobellogold.com

directory

Our London directory has everything you need to get the best out of the city, from annual events to finding the best hotels and places to stay in all categories. There are suggestions for seeking out additional sightseeing attractions such as museums, art galleries, parks and gardens not included in earlier chapters. You'll also find ideas for further reading, listings of popular web sites and local newspapers as well as a special feature on how to understand the natives.

Key to Icons

Room Service	@	Business Centre
Restaurant	Health Centre
Fully Licensed Bar	✹	Air Conditioning
En-suite Bathroom	P	Parking

Hotels

@ Business Centre
Health Centre
✹ Air Conditioning
P Parking

Museums

👭 Toilets
♿ Disabled Facilities
Refreshments
Free Admission
Guided Tours

Places to Stay

From bastions of old-world antique luxury to the latest modernist masterpieces, from comfortable to fashionable, cluttered to minimalis exorbitant to bargain, 24-hour roo service to self-catering – London h hotels to suit all tastes and budget Here are some of the best. All pric are inclusive of VAT (15 per cent).

Luxury

Brown's £££-££££ ❷ 4D

A fine hotel that exudes a refined country-house ambience with oak panelling, grandfather clocks and leather armchairs. *34 Albemarle Street W1, T: 020 7493 6020, www.brownshotel.com*

> **Price** (per double room)
> **£** budget (under £100)
> **££** moderate (£100-£200)
> **£££** expensive (£200-£300)
> **££££** luxury (£300+)

harlotte Street Hotel £££ ❷ 1E

ver-so-fashionable, the public
ooms offer a pastiche of old-world
nglish style with dark wood
anelling and soft-glow lighting
hile the bedrooms have every
odern convenience. *18 Charlotte
reet W1, T: 020 7806 2000,
ww.firmdale.com*

ovent Garden Hotel £££-££££
❶3G

op-of-the-range luxury combined
ith old-style elegance – four-poster
eds, mahogany and marble right in
e heart of London. *10 Monmouth
reet WC2, T: 020 7806 1000,
ww.firmdale.com*

orchester ££££ ❷5B

1930s, Art Deco-style hotel filled
ith triple-glazed, gold-leafed,
lvet-cushioned opulence it is the
oice of discerning film stars.
Park Lane W1, T: 020 7629 8888,
ww.dorchesterhotel.com

The Ritz ££££ ❷5D

Famous for its teas (*see p.45*), this is
the eponymous luxury hotel; a
byword for glamourous living, it is
decorated in lavish rococo style with
marble, gilt bronze and gold leaf.
*150 Piccadilly W1, T: 020 7493 8181,
www.theritzlondon.com*

Chic

The Academy ££ ❷1F

A collection of stylish and
comfortable townhouses, with a
peaceful garden, near the British
Museum and Tottenham Court
Road. The individually designed
rooms have extras such as personal
business cards and crisp Egyptian
cotton linen. *21 Gower Street,
Bloomsbury SW7, T: 020 7631 4115,
www.theetoncollection.com*

The Cumberland £££ ❷3A

Original artworks and sculptures
adorn this surreal minimalist hotel.
Top DJs play in the Carbon Room

while Gary Rhodes tickles tastebuds
in the flagship restaurant. *Great
Cumberland Place W1,
T: 0870 333 9280, www.guoman.com*

The Gore ££-£££ ❶4B

Atmospheric Victorian hotel offering
a combination of antique styling and
modern chic. *190 Queen's Gate SW7,
T: 020 7584 6601, www.gorehotel.com*

Indigo ££ ❶3C

London's first hip Indigo boutique
hotel opened in December 2008.
The 64 rooms are revamped
throughout the year to keep the
design fresh. *16 London Street W2,
T: 020 7706 4444,
www.hipaddington.com*

Sanderson £££-££££ ❶3E

Its super-smart surreal minimalist
interior is a hip, ultra-cool style-mag
favourite, especially the 24m (80ft)
Long Bar. Rooms have glass walls
with flowing curtains and the
dreamy white theme continues into

the spa and bathhouse. *50 Berners Street W1, T: 020 7300 1400, www.sandersonlondon.com*

Portobello ££-£££ ● 3A

Cosy rooms with masses of Victoriana and colonial-style chic furnishings. *22 Stanley Gardens W11, T: 020 7727 2777, www.portobello-hotel.co.uk*

Tophams ££-£££ ● 5D

Re-opened after a £4 million refurbishment in 2008, this four-star boutique hotel offers five different bedroom schemes. *24-32 Ebury Street SW1, T: 020 7730 3313, www.zolahotels.com/tophams*

Affordable style

Abbey Court ££ ● 4A

Bedrooms with an antique feel and bathrooms of marble and brass. *20 Pembridge Gardens W2, T: 020 7221 7518, www.abbeycourthotel.co.uk*

ANdAZ ££ ● 3H

Within a 19th-century building, you'll find 21st-century, cool, contemporary design. This hip hangout offers five restaurants, four bars and wi-fi in rooms. *40 Liverpool Street EC2, T: 020 7961 1234, www.london.liverpoolstreet.andaz.com*

Durrants ££ ❷ 2B

All dark woods and leather contrasted with clean, fresh furnishings inside this former 18th-century coaching inn combine with calm, careful service. *George Street W1, T: 020 7935 8131, www.durrantshotel.co.uk*

Mayflower £-££ ● 5B

Oozing an elegant East-meets-West style with hand-carved beds, Egyptian cotton sheets and oriental furnishings: a great-value hotel close to Earl's Court. *26-28 Trebovir Road SW5, T: 020 7370 0991, www.mayflowerhotel.co.uk*

Park Plaza County Hall £-££ ● 5F

Modern, chic hotel close to the live South Bank and County Hall. Room feature kitchenette, microwave and tea/coffee maker. *1 Addington Stree SE1, T: 020 7021 1800, www.parkplaza.com*

Pavilion Hotel £ ● 3C

Eccentric hotel near Paddington station with themed rooms such as Casablanca Nights, Highland Fling and Honky Tonk Afro, popular with visiting glitterati. *34-36 Sussex Gardens W2, T: 020 7262 0905, www.pavilionhoteluk.com*

Inexpensive

base2stay™ £-££ ● 5B

The clean, simply furnished, yet elegantly designed apartments offer incredible value. All have kitchenett and rooms for one person or family rooms. *25 Courtfield Gardens SW5, T: 020 7244 2255, www.base2stay.co*

easyHotel £ ① 5B

Compact rooms with basic facilities (many without windows) but all en suite at budget prices. As with many easy-branded items, the earlier you book, the less you pay. *14 Lexham Gardens W8, http://easyhotel.com*

Edward Lear Hotel £ ② 3A

A cheerful, family-run hotel occupies the former home of Victorian limerick writer, Edward Lear; close to Oxford Street. *28-30 Seymour Street W1, T: 020 7402 5401, www.edlear.co.uk*

Museums

Main entries in See it *pp.2-15*.

British Library ① 1E

Includes the Lindisfarne Gospels and a copy of the Magna Carta. *Open 9.30am-6pm Mon, Wed-Fri, 9.30am-8pm Tue, 9.30am-5pm Sat, 11am-5pm Sun. 96 Euston Road N1, T: 020 7412 7332, www.bl.uk*

Clink Prison Museum ① 4G

Exhibits on punishment and torture in medieval prisons. *Adm. Open 10am-6pm Mon-Fri, 10am-9pm Sat-Sun. 1 Clink Street SE1, T: 020 7403 0900, www.clink.co.uk*

London Canal Museum ① 1F

The history of London's waterways. *Adm. Open 10am-4.30pm Tue-Sun. New Wharf Road N1, T: 020 7713 0836, www.canalmuseum.org.uk*

MCC Museum ① 1C

The spiritual home of cricket. *Tours daily. Adm. St John's Wood Road NW8, T: 020 7616 8500, www.lords.org*

National Army Museum ① 6C

History of the British Army, with uniforms and model soldiers. *Open 10am-5.30pm daily. Royal Hospital Road SW3, T: 020 7730 0717, www.national-army-museum.ac.uk*

Old Operating Theatre Museum & Herb Garret ① 4H

The world's oldest surviving operating theatre (1822), where gruesome pre-anaesthetic operations were carried out. *Open 10.30am-5pm daily. 9A St Thomas Street SE1, T: 020 7188 2679, www.thegarret.org.uk*

Sir John Soane's Museum ① 3F

Bizarre collection of art, antiques and curiosities collected in the 18th and 19th centuries by Sir John Soane. *Open 10am-5pm Tue-Sat (till 9pm 1st Tue of each month). 13 Lincoln's Inn Fields WC2, T: 020 7405 2107, www.soane.org*

Wallace Collection ② 2B

Collection of 18th-century French paintings and Sèvres porcelain. *Open 10am-5pm daily. Hertford House, Manchester Square W1, T: 020 7935 0687, www.wallacecollection.org*

directory

59

Galleries

Find main entries in See it pp.2-15.

ICA Gallery ② 5F
👫 ♿ 🍴

Varied programme of temporary modern art exhibitions. *Adm. Open 12noon-1am Tue-Sat, 12noon-10.30pm Sun, 12noon-11pm Mon. The Mall SW1, T: 020 7930 3647, www.ica.org.uk*

Guildhall Art Gallery ❶ 3G
👫 ♿ 🏛

Displays the City of London's art. *Adm. Open 10am-5pm Mon-Sat, 12noon-4pm Sun. Gresham Street EC2, T: 020 7606 3030, www.cityoflondon.gov.uk*

Royal Academy of Arts ② 4D
👫 ♿ 🍴

Temporary exhibitions: its annual Summer Exhibition of contemporary art runs from June to August. *Adm. Open 10am-6pm Sat-Thu, 10am-10pm Fri. Burlington House, Piccadilly W1, T: 020 7300 8000, www.royalacademy.org.uk*

Monuments

Banqueting House ② 6G
👫

Originally part of Whitehall Palace, the sovereign's residence from 1530 to 1698, with elaborate ceiling fresco painted by Rubens. *Adm. Open 10am-5pm Mon-Sat. Whitehall SW1, T: 0844 482 7799, www.hrp.org.uk*

HMS Belfast ❶ 4H
👫 ♿ 🍴 🏛

Enormous World War II battlecruiser, now a floating museum. *Adm. Open 10am-6pm daily Mar-Oct, 10am-5pm daily Nov-Feb. Morgan's Lane, Tooley Street SE1, T: 020 7940 6300, hmsbelfast.iwm.org.uk*

Parks & Gardens

Battersea Park ❶ 6D

Boating lake, café, festival gardens, a pagoda and children's zoo. *Battersea SW11, www.batterseapark.org*

Chelsea Physic Garden ❶ 6C

Peaceful apothecaries' research garden. *Adm. Open 12noon-5pm Wed, Thu, Fri 12noon-6pm, Sun Apr-Oct. 66 Royal Hospital Road SW3, T: 020 7352 5646, www.chelseaphysicgarden.co.uk*

Christchurch Greyfriars ❶ 3G

Delightful rose garden planted on the former site of Sir Christopher Wren's church. *Newgate Street EC1, www.christchurchtower.com*

Green Park ② 6C-7D

Peaceful mature green park. *The Mall SW1, www.royalparks.gov.uk*

Holland Park ❶ 4A

Manicured park with an orangery, a Japanese watergarden, peacocks and a theatre (see p.31). *Kensington W8, www.rbkc.gov.uk*

Lincoln's Inn Fields ❶ 3F

17th-century garden filled with lawyers (extremely quiet considering its location), and the largest public square in London. *Holborn WC2.*

Regent's Park ❶ 1C-2D

Boating lake, tennis courts, café, open-air summer theatre (see p.30) and London Zoo (see p.8). *NW1, www.royalparks.gov.uk.*

Annual Events

January
London Parade (New Year's Day).
www.londonparade.co.uk

January-February
Chinese New Year Festival.
Chinatown WC1.

March
Oxford & Cambridge Boat Race on
the Thames. www.theboatrace.org

April
London Marathon run around
Greenwich (see p.5) and the Isle of
Dogs. www.london-marathon.co.uk
Queen's Birthday Royal Gun Salute
(21st, 12noon). Hyde Park, Tower.

May
Chelsea Flower Show the Chelsea
Physic Garden. www.rhs.org.uk

June-August
Royal Academy Summer Exhibition
(see left).
Trooping the Colour (2nd Saturday
June). The Queen's official birthday.
**Wimbledon Lawn Tennis
Championships** Two weeks Jun-Jul.

July-September
The Proms more than 70 concerts,
(see p.31). www.bbc.co.uk/proms

August
Notting Hill Carnival (August Bank
Holiday Sun). Europe's largest.
T: 020 7727 0072, www.lnhc.org.uk

October
**Pearly Kings and Queens' Harvest
Festival** where East Enders are
smothered in buttons (second
Sunday in October).
www.pearlysociety.co.uk

November
Guy Fawkes/Bonfire Night (5th).
Firework displays throughout city.
Lord Mayor's Show (second
Saturday in November, starts at
11am). EC1, www.lordmayorshow.org

December
The Christmas Lights. Trafalgar
Square, Oxford and Regent Streets,
and **New Year's Eve Celebrations**
(31st). Trafalgar Square.

Listings

See the **What's On** section p.28.

Newspapers

Metro is free daily Mon-Fri from tube
stations. The London Evening
Standard appears late afternoon
Mon-Fri. The Times and the Guardian
are daily Mon-Sat.

Reading

Take the Kids…London –
Joseph Fullman, Cadogan Guides.

London: the Biography –
Peter Akroyd, Vintage.
London as a living organism.

Oliver Twist – **Charles Dickens**.
One of the many London-set texts
by the great 19th-century novelist.

Websites

Visit London
www.visitlondon.com

LondonTown.com
Massive discounts on hotels and
accommodation as well as
information on sightseeing.
www.londontown.com

speak it

Here are a few local words and phrases to spare any blushes during your stay in London.

All-too-common UK/US confusions
bank holiday – national holiday
Boxing Day – the day after Christmas Day (national holiday)
chemist – drugstore
dress circle (theatre) – first balcony
fags – cigarettes
fortnight – two weeks
interval – intermission
letter box or pillar box – mail-box
lift – elevator
loo/WC – toilet
rucksack – backpack
stalls – theatre seats
tap – faucet
torch – flashlight

Around London
cab rank – taxi-stand
return ticket – round trip
pavement – sidewalk
subway – pedestrian underpass
tube – subway

Babies and children
dummy – pacifier
nappy – diaper
pram – baby-carriage
pushchair – child's stroller

Clothes
anorak – windbreaker (slang: nerd)
dressing gown – robe
jumper, pullover, woolly – sweater
knickers – ladies' underpants
pants – underpants
trainers – sneakers
trousers – pants
vest – undershirt

Money
coppers – 1p and 2p coins
quid – a pound
fiver – a five pound note
tenner – a ten pound note
hole-in-the-wall – ATM

Slang
bird – woman (impolite)
bloke – man
bog – toilet
copper – policeman
fag – cigarette
knackered – extremely tired
spend a penny – go to the toilet

Cockney rhyming slang

This famous east-London dialect where words and phrases are substituted with rhyming alternatives is, despite its renown, rarely used. You may hear some of these:

Adam and Eve – believe
apples and pears – stairs
Barnet (fair) – hair
boracic (lint) – skint
brass tacks – facts
butcher's (hook) – look
china (plate) – mate, friend
cobbler's (awls) – balls, rubbish
cream-crackered – knackered, tired
daisy roots – boots
dog (and bone) – phone
dustbin lids – kids
frog and toad – road
loaf (of bread) – head
mince pies – eyes
Pete Tong – wrong
Rosy (Lea) – tea
rub-a-dub – pub
Ruby (Murray) – curry
Scarpa (flow) – go
titfer (tat) – hat
trouble 'n' strife – wife
whistle (and flute) – suit (clothes)

Fiona Quinn. Updated by
Kathryn Liston.
Revision management by
Cambridge Publishing
Management Ltd.
Pictures © Compass Maps
Ltd and John Heseltine
Archive except Alan Copson
(pp.1, 3, 5, 7, 10, 14, 17, 18,
19, 21, 22, 30, 31, 40, 45,
50, 51, 52, 53, 54). Corbis,
Dali Universe (p.6),
Kensington Palace (p.7),
London Aquarium (p.8),
Museum of London (p.9), Nik
Milner/ Shakespeare's Globe
(p.12), Shutterstock/Robert
Gooch (p.11), Tate Modern
(p.13), Getty/Photodisc
(p.49), Tower Bridge
Experience (p.14), Michael
Walker/Troika (p.51), V&A
Museum (p.15), Dean and
Chapter of Westminster
(p.15), B (p.23), Hamley's
(p.25), Jazz Café (p.33),
Comedy Café (p.33).
Cover Images: Clive Sawyer/
PCL and David Noble/PCL.
This PopOut insideout
product, its associated
machinery and format use,
whether singular or
integrated within other
products, is subject to
worldwide patents granted &
pending, including
EP1417665,
CN ZL02819864.6 &
CN ZL200620006638.7.
All rights reserved including
design, copyright, trademark
and associated intellectual
property rights. PopOut is a
registered trademark and is
produced under license by
Compass Maps Ltd. 7927

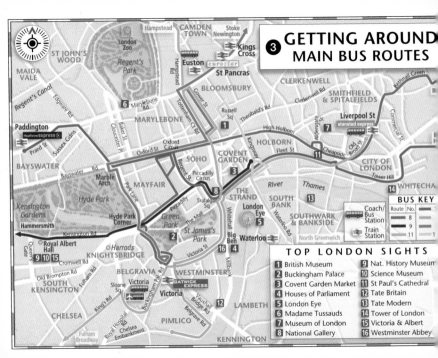